Focus on Babies:

How-tos and What-to-dos when Caring for Infants

Also by Jennifer Karnopp:

Family Child Care Basics: Advice, Activities, and Information to Create a Professional Program

Elementos de un Cuidado de Niños Hogareño: Consejos, Actividades e Información para Crear un Programa Profesional

Focus on Toddlers: How-tos and What-to-dos when Caring for Toddlers and Twos

GH10516
A Gryphon House Book

FOCUS ON

How-tos and What-to-dos when Caring for Infants

BABIES

Jennifer Karnopp

Illustrations by Deb Johnson

Gryphon House, Inc.
Lewisville, NC

Published by Gryphon House, Inc.
PO Box 10, Lewisville, NC 27023
800-638-0928; 877-638-7576 (fax)
Visit us on the web at www.gryphonhouse.com.

Cover photograph courtesy of iStockphoto.
Illustrations by Deb Johnson.
Photographs courtesy of iStockphoto.

Library of Congress Cataloging-in-Publication Data
Karnopp, Jennifer.
  Focus on babies : how-tos and what-to-dos when caring for infants / by Jennifer Karnopp ; illustrations by Deb Johnson.
     p. cm.
  Includes index.
  ISBN 978-0-87659-379-0
  1. Child care. 2. Infants--Care. 3. Early childhood education. 4. Child care services. I. Title.
  HQ778.5.K373 2012
  649'.1--dc23
                         2012004435

Bulk Purchase
Gryphon House books are available for special premiums and sales promotions as well as for fund-raising use. Special editions or book excerpts also can be created to specifications. For details, contact the Director of Marketing at Gryphon House.

Disclaimer
Gryphon House, Inc. cannot be held responsible for damage, mishap, or injury incurred during the use of or because of activities in this book. Appropriate and reasonable caution and adult supervision of children involved in activities and corresponding to the age and capability of each child involved is recommended at all times. Do not leave children unattended at any time. Observe safety and caution at all times.

Contents

Introduction

Purpose

A quality learning environment is important for the healthy development of all young children, even infants. But the elements of a quality environment are not the same for every age. What works for preschoolers does not always work with toddlers, and what might be appropriate for toddlers is not necessarily the best arrangement for infants. In this book you will find information and ideas to help you create a quality early learning program specifically for the infants in your care. While safety is always an important concern of any program, safety issues, rules, and regulations are not the focus of this book. Instead, we will take a look at the many elements that make up a quality program. We will explore ideas for your physical space, your daily routines, your relationships and interactions with babies and their families, and the experiences you create. After reading this book, you will be able to create a center-based program perfectly suited to meet the unique needs of infants and their families, and suited to you, the caregiver, as well.

Developmentally Appropriate Practice

As a caregiver, you may feel pressured to "teach" infants or focus on their brain development. Without a doubt, infants will benefit from a program that meets their developmental needs, but keep in mind that their needs are unique. Resist the temptation to model your program after a preschool classroom. Infants are not tiny preschoolers, and thinking of them as such just is not developmentally appropriate.

Infants' muscles, senses, and brains are all developing rapidly. They spend their days just trying to make sense of their own bodies and the world around them. From the moment that they are born, babies are constantly making new discoveries and problem solving. This takes all of their energy and focus. To help support infants as they grow and develop, we need to know them as individuals, to understand where they are developmentally, and to encourage their explorations.

Creating a developmentally appropriate environment for infants means that you support them as they practice and perfect discoveries that they have already made (the skills they have at their current level of development) and then encourage them to problem-solve and try new things (to push themselves toward the next level of development). In other words, developmentally appropriate practice is the art of encouraging children to perfect old skills and explore new ones without getting bored or being frustrated.

To help you create a developmentally appropriate infant program, we will first explore your role as the caregiver. We will take a look at the elements that make up a good infant environment, including how to set up your space and how to plan and evaluate your program. We will explore all that goes into a child-centered daily routine and give you information on infant growth and development. You will also find some basic information on working with children who have special needs.

A young child develops and grows as a whole child, meaning that all areas of development are interconnected. As a baby learns to grasp objects and bang, shake or mouth those objects, she is developing motor skills. When she hears her caregiver name the object that she grabs, she is developing language skills. When she smiles at her caregiver as she shakes the object and receives a smile in return, her caregiver is encouraging social skills and emotional development. The baby then takes in all of these experiences and information to develop a better understanding of the object. It is soft and easy to grab. It is safe to grab. There is a word that describes the object, and when I explore the object, my caregiver smiles at me. Improved abilities in one area of development enable a child to further explore another area. And when a child can better explore the world, she can better understand the world. For this reason, the rest of this book is devoted to activities that will help you meet the needs of infants in all areas of their development. Here, the words activity and experience are used interchangeably to mean a planned, open-ended experience. The activities are divided into four sections.

- ◌ **Social and Emotional:** experiences that encourage social interactions and bonding and promote healthy emotional development
- ◌ **Language:** experiences that promote early language development and communication skills
- ◌ **Motor:** experiences that develop both fine and gross motor skills
- ◌ **Sensory:** experiences that encourage sensory (touch, taste, smell, sound, sight) awareness

Each activity also includes a "tips" section where you will find ideas for natural, playful ways to incorporate cognitive development, as well as other developmental areas, into each activity. We have not included a separate activity section for cognitive development, because an infant's cognitive development depends on the development of each of the above areas. When an infant grabs an item and explores it with her mouth, she is using motor skills and sensory skills to begin to understand the objects in her environment. Coming to that understanding is a cognitive skill. Instead of a dedicated cognitive section, you will discover that the exploratory nature of each activity gives infants all kinds of opportunities to develop age-appropriate thinking skills.

A Guide to the Activities

The activities or experiences in this book are divided into four different developmental areas. Each activity's developmental area is marked in the upper right-hand corner of the page, and each has a corresponding icon. The upper right-hand corner also lets you know the appropriate ages for the activity, where it will work best, and how long to expect to prepare for it. Keep in mind, the ages are just approximations, so do not feel bound by them. All children are different. You know the infants you are working with. Just take care not to push a child to do activities when she is not interested. Watch for signs that she may need a break or may not be ready for structured activities. Reactions such as turning away from an activity, fussing, or showing a lack of interest are all signs that the activity is not a good fit at this moment. Pay attention to these signals from baby, and stop the activity for the time being. You can always try again later.

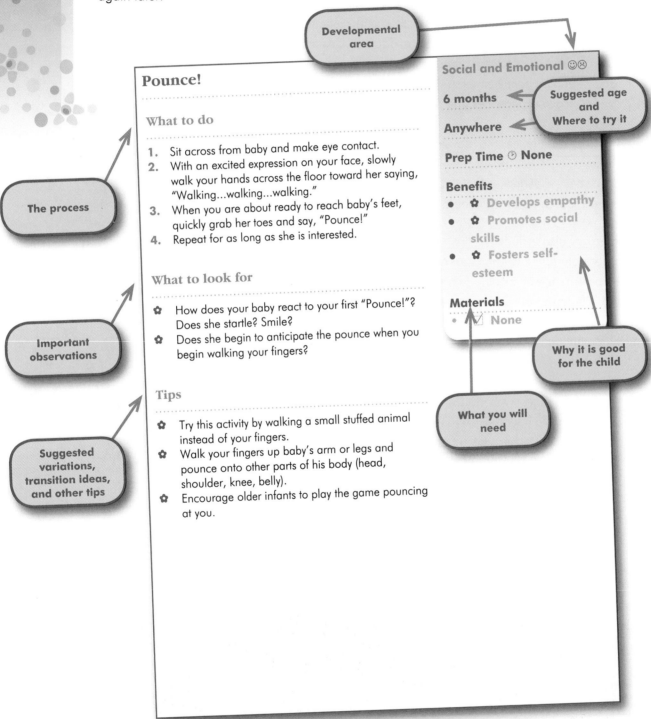

Developmental area

Pounce!

What to do

1. Sit across from baby and make eye contact.
2. With an excited expression on your face, slowly walk your hands across the floor toward her saying, "Walking...walking...walking."
3. When you are about ready to reach baby's feet, quickly grab her toes and say, "Pounce!"
4. Repeat for as long as she is interested.

What to look for

✿ How does your baby react to your first "Pounce!"? Does she startle? Smile?
✿ Does she begin to anticipate the pounce when you begin walking your fingers?

Tips

✿ Try this activity by walking a small stuffed animal instead of your fingers.
✿ Walk your fingers up baby's arm or legs and pounce onto other parts of his body (head, shoulder, knee, belly).
✿ Encourage older infants to play the game pouncing at you.

Social and Emotional ☺☹

6 months

Anywhere

Prep Time ⏱ None

Benefits
● ✿ Develops empathy
● ✿ Promotes social skills
● ✿ Fosters self-esteem

Materials
● ☑ None

The process

Important observations

Suggested variations, transition ideas, and other tips

Suggested age and Where to try it

Why it is good for the child

What you will need

Chapter 1:
The Role of the Caregiver

An infant room is very different from any other early childhood classroom. The furniture is different, the routine is different, and the activities are different. It makes sense then that the role of the caregiver is also very different. From the moment an infant is brought into the room, a caregiver needs to respond to the needs of that child. Infants spend every waking moment exploring their environment and learning about the world around them. For them, every experience is a learning experience. As a caregiver, your role is to get to know the infants in your care and to create a warm, safe environment that will meet their emotional needs and encourage their explorations. To be a good infant caregiver, you need to be a skilled child observer and willing to make personal connections with babies and their families.

Developing Attachment

The most important developmental step an infant must take is to feel emotionally attached to the adult caring for him. This feeling of attachment helps him to develop trust and gives him a stable foundation on which to build a variety of other skills. Most infants naturally develop attachment to their family members, and this bond is extremely important. However, an infant can feel attached to more than one person and should also feel attached to her caregiver. After all, you are the person responding to her needs while her family members are away. All caregivers should set the important goal of promoting this feeling of attachment in their child care settings.

Group size and the child-to-caregiver ratio have a tremendous impact on a caregiver's ability to create bonds with her infants. If the group is too large, or if children are cared for by too many different people, infants will not be responded to consistently and sensitively. Each state has its own child-to-caregiver ratio guidelines for licensing, but you may also want to consider following these recommended minimum child-to-caregiver ratio guidelines that are required for accreditation by the National Association for the Education of Young Children (NAEYC, 2007):

Age	Group size: 6	Group size: 8	Group size: 10	Group size: 12
Birth to 15 months	1:3	1:4	x	x
12–28 months	1:3	1:4	1:4	1:4

Another problem often encountered in child care centers is staff absences or high staff turnover. Children will be cared for inconsistently and have a hard time bonding to their caregiver if they are cared for by many different people. Consistency is extremely important to an infant's healthy development. Being cared for by the same person consistently allows an infant to develop trust (attachment). Trust gives an infant a sense of confidence that his caregiver will always be there when he needs her. This confidence encourages babies to explore their world, and this exploration then leads to healthy development.

Primary Caregiver System

To address issues of consistency, consider a primary caregiver system. Here one caregiver is assigned to a few infants, but she has the support of a team. For example, a group of three caregivers shares a room and works together as a team. Each caregiver has two or three infants for whom she is the primary caregiver. Because she is almost always the person responding to her assigned infants, each caregiver comes to know her children's temperaments, likes, and dislikes very well. Each has only two or three babies to focus on, so she is usually able to respond quickly and consistently. This does not mean that an infant's primary caregiver is her only caregiver. If a situation arises where a primary caregiver is unable to attend to one of her children, the two other caregivers on the team can work together to attend to the child in need while still managing the rest of the group. Ideally, a child will have the same primary caregiver throughout her stay at your center. When a group of 18-month-olds is ready to move on to the two-year-old room, their primary caregiver would move along with them. This greatly reduces the stress of yearly transitions for children, family members, and teachers.

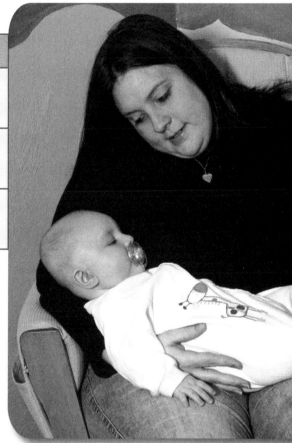

Primary Caregiver Responsibilities
✿ Know the infants (likes and dislikes, health issues, developmental stages, temperaments, schedules).
✿ Be a family advocate (sensitive to family culture and values, address family members' needs and concerns).
✿ Facilitate communication (daily communication with family members, update staff on child issues).

The primary caregiver system has many advantages. It is great for infants because it allows caregivers to develop strong bonds with their primary infants. Caregivers learn to understand the individual needs of each child and begin to identify each child's unique way of communicating. When infants are responded to quickly and consistently, they learn the important lesson that they have the ability to affect their world. This is a good thing. Attachment and trust lay the foundation for independence as babies become toddlers. Caregivers participating in this type of a system also get to know the other infants in the group. This group bonding helps the children get some consistency even when their primary caregiver is absent.

The primary caregiver system is also good for caregivers. Trying to meet the needs of a screaming infant can be tiring, stressful, and frustrating. The job is a lot easier when you really know the child, understand his ways of communicating, and feel bonded to that child. A close relationship can only come from caring for and paying attention to the same child over a period of time. Also, bonding with an infant feels good. It creates positive feelings that make the work of providing care more pleasurable. Finally, caregivers working in a team situation have the immediate support of colleagues. Together they can talk about ideas or concerns and are in a better position to address issues quickly.

Even families benefit from the primary caregiver system. Not only are primary caregivers very familiar with the temperaments and daily activities of the infants in their care, they should also be very familiar with the culture and values of their infants' families. Primary caregivers are child and family advocates and should inform and update other caregivers on important issues such as medications, cultural beliefs, and other health or family concerns. A team of caregivers can also work together to ensure that each has a chance to fill out daily communications or write brief anecdotal records for each infant, helping families to stay informed.

Interacting with Infants

When interacting with infants, always take the time to involve them. Too often babies are handled as objects. They are abruptly moved from crib to high chair or from play mat to changing table without a word. Instead, treat a young child as you would an elderly person who needs your assistance. Let her know what you are doing before you do it. Involve her. Soon you will see infants reacting to your words and beginning to reach for you when you tell them you are going to pick them up.

Without a doubt, you will spend most of the day meeting infants' daily needs. Diapering, feeding, burping, and soothing infants may seem time-consuming and mundane, but these routine activities can be wonderful educational opportunities. For example, think about a typical diapering experience.

Ari is a six-month-old infant who is lying on his belly inspecting a small crumb he has noticed on his mat. As he leans to poke it with his finger, his caregiver, Liz, suddenly picks him up and walks to the changing table. Ari protests as he is pulled away from the crumb. Liz lays him down and taps a mobile, making it move. Ari stares, captivated by the motion, and quickly settles down. Liz removes the old diaper, cleans him, and places a new diaper under him. She works quickly and quietly until she begins talking with a nearby colleague. Ari is watching her now, but she does not notice, and without turning to face him, she grabs his legs and repositions him on the diaper, then finishes the job. Liz quickly looks to make sure the diaper is on properly, then picks up the child and returns him to his original spot, still focused on her conversation with the other caregiver. Ari looks around with big eyes, and then notices a nearby toy, which he begins to reach for.

Tummy time: beginning from birth a baby should be placed on his tummy for brief periods at least twice a day*. As he gets more comfortable with this position, increase the length of each tummy time period. Tummy time helps infants to develop the muscles needed to lift their heads and upper bodies, and to explore the movements that will eventually lead to rolling over and crawling.
*Recommended by the National Institute for Child and Human Development

Contrast that with this diapering experience: Cara holds her arms out and says the name of six-month-old Polly, who is lying on her tummy inspecting a crumb on the mat. Cara tells Polly that it is time for a diaper change. Polly turns her head to Cara and smiles. Cara then picks up Polly and places her on the changing table. As she changes the baby's diaper, she talks to her. Polly looks at Cara and focuses her gaze on Cara's face and mouth. She babbles and coos in response to Cara's words. Cara watches Polly's expressions as she tells her what she is doing. She asks for Polly's help, saying, "Lift your legs, sweetie. I need to slide this diaper under you. Move your hands so I can clean you." Cara holds a wipe above Polly's belly, and the baby reaches for it. Sometimes Polly responds as Cara would like, and sometimes Cara needs to move her. Cara finishes putting on the new diaper, quickly wipes her hands clean, and then tells Polly she is finished as she holds her hands out. Polly reaches for Cara. Cara picks her up and places her back in her original spot. Polly notices a nearby toy right away and grasps for it.

Instead of simply changing Polly's diaper to get the job done, Cara used this one-on-one time as an opportunity to strengthen bonds. Polly listened to Cara as she spoke and maybe even responded, developing language skills. Polly lifted her legs and reached for the wipe Cara held, developing motor skills. Cara turned a simple diaper change into a learning experience.

Good caregivers should do the following:
✿ Smile, talk to, and babble with infants

✿ Be involved with play:
  ✿ Retrieve toys, play peek-a-boo and other games
  ✿ Look for toys, games, or experiences that ignite interest

✿ Change infants' positions, and help them discover new possibilities when they are bored
✿ Feed infants when they are hungry, and avoid using food to soothe

✿ Meet infants' emotional needs:
  ✿ Sing to and rock infants when they are tired
  ✿ Hold them when they feel sad or loving
  ✿ Notice when children need quiet and alone time

✿ Express delight when noticing new skills like creeping, dropping, and making new sounds

When you are not busy attending to the daily needs of the infants in your care, be a child observer. Watch each infant at play. Respond to each child, but do not always initiate activities. Create situations where they can explore objects or challenge their abilities, but allow them to do their own exploring and challenging. Remember, they do it naturally! This does not mean that you should not play with them. Do! Spending time with an infant when you are not working to meet an immediate need helps the child to feel valued. But be aware of the difference between playing with infants and controlling the play. Also, do not be afraid of giving infants some alone time. Even babies need to learn to self-soothe or problem-solve. Draw upon your knowledge of each child to help you decide when to step in to keep an infant from becoming bored or frustrated.

Most important, be consistent! It is through consistency that babies learn cause and effect, arguably an infant's most important lesson. This early understanding of the relationship between their actions (crying, smiling, cooing) and your behavior (feeding, smiling, cuddling) is extremely important for healthy development. It also helps to build a sense of trust and security, which will encourage independence as the child grows.

Handling "Bad" Behavior

Young infants are not capable of behaving badly. They cry to communicate their needs or because they are experiencing discomfort. They do not manipulate. Older infants are a bit more complex. They are beginning to test limits and will behave badly for a variety of reasons.

Like young infants, older infants may cry or act out in an attempt to communicate a need that is not being met. They may be tired, hungry, need more attention, or feel overstimulated. To stop the behavior, try to identify and fulfill these needs.

Older infants may also act out when they do not know how to express their feelings. An older infant may feel angry that another child took a toy away, or hurt when her family member leaves for the day. Help children to identify these feelings and validate them. It is okay to cry when we feel sad. If a child's behavior is not appropriate, such as hitting another child to express anger, calmly stop the behavior and show her a more appropriate way to express her feelings.

As older infants develop, they begin to gain a sense of self. They test boundaries. Be prepared for this and make sure that your environment is set up in a way that ensures off-limits places are truly off-limits. A gate blocking infant access to stairs will prevent you from having to physically remove an infant from the stairs over and over again. Be clear and consistent with the limits you impose. Young children test boundaries to make sure they are there.

No matter what the source of an infant's behavior problems, punishment does not belong in an infant environment. Calm persistence and consistency and redirection are much more successful ways of changing behavior. If this does not work, or if the situation calls for more direct action, firm but gentle physical restraint is appropriate. For example, if Eliza is about to hit Noah on the head with a block, firmly grab Eliza's arm and gently remove the block as you explain to her that she was going to hurt Noah. Avoid shaming or belittling young children. They are learning the rules of society. Children are not born with social skills. These skills develop through interactions and experiences.

Trying to manage a group of expressive and impulsive infants can be frustrating! You are only human, and you may need to take a moment to remove yourself from a particularly aggravating situation. Never try to control children with anger. Young children are excellent mimics. Watching your behavior is one of the ways they learn. If you try to control them with anger, expect that they will try to do the same to you.

Involving Families

Quality child care programs not only serve children but their families as well. Family members of infants are going through what can be a difficult and stressful time in their lives. They may be first-time parents, unsure of what to do and overwhelmed by their new lives. Even experienced parents may be suffering from lack of sleep, concerned by older siblings' reactions to the new baby, or stressed by the new financial strain of an infant.

It is also common for family members to have mixed emotions about leaving their infant in the care of others. They may feel guilty for leaving their infant or concerned about whether or not their child's needs will be met while they are away. Some family members may feel uncomfortable in a child care setting, not knowing how to act. They may see you as an expert on children and may feel intimidated. All family members need to feel that they are part of their child's day, even when they cannot physically be there. This connection is not only important for family members, it is also important for the child. It is up to you to make that happen.

As a caregiver you have to perform a balancing act. Families want to feel that you are competent, but they do not want to feel that you know more about how to care for their child than they do. They want their child to like you and enjoy his time in your care, but they do not want to feel that their child likes you more than them. Families want to know what their child does each day, but some families may not want to hear that they missed their child's first word or other important milestones. You can address these concerns by being sensitive to these potentially conflicting feelings. Instead of announcing that their baby said the word more today, consider asking families to listen for the word because you thought you may have heard it. Be supportive and reassuring to family members. These mixed feelings are normal and go hand in hand with sharing care. Let them know that they are the most important people in their child's life.

To help family members feel at ease, welcome, and involved, think about the following aspects of your program:
✿ The entrance: Is it welcoming and comfortable?
✿ The infant area: Does it include and reflect the children's families and cultures? Does it encourage families to sit and watch their infants at play?
✿ Communication: Do family members receive a consistent and accurate idea of how their child's day has been? How do they learn about upcoming events or get information about parenting issues?

The entrance and the infant area of your program really do set the tone and visually reinforce the values of your program. However, they will be discussed more in the next section of this book. Here we will give you ideas on how to communicate with families in a way that makes them feel involved.

The best way to really communicate with families is to talk one-on-one. However, the end of the day is always hectic, and talking with each family member is easier said than done. One simple way to communicate the basics of each child's day is to have a clipboard for each child, with a chart that can be filled out easily by the primary caregiver every day. You will find two examples of this kind of chart at the end of this section. Make these charts easily accessible to caregivers during the day, and then hang them in the same place each afternoon so that family members can see them easily. Family members in a rush can pick up their baby and have a quick look to see how the day went. Those who have more time can have a look at their child's chart and wait for you to become available if they have a question, concern, or just want to hear more. Do keep track of which family members you have spoken with, so that you will know which family members you need to make the effort to talk to in the future. (Refer to form on page 15.) Make sure to have one-on-one conversations with each family member on a regular basis. Keep these daily charts in each child's file for future reference. They can be useful if you want to identify a pattern of behavior or look back on past experiences that you provided.

Another great way to make family members feel like a part of your program is to take a lot of photographs. Unlike the daily charts, photographs capture the spirit of your program. Display the pictures in the entrance and in other areas. These photos are a great way to draw apprehensive family members in and get busy family members to slow down a moment. All family members love to see their children engaged and happy while they are away. This can be especially helpful to family members who have difficulty with separation. Be sure to change the pictures often. Infants grow quickly, and you want to send the signal that your program is fresh and current.

Daily Chart

Name	Date

I had a great time	I need more

I ate   ◯ All of my lunch
      ◯ About half
      ◯ Some
	I enjoyed my bottles.
	     a.m. _____
	     p.m. _____

I napped
     a.m. _____
     p.m. _____
     a.m. _____
     p.m. _____
	I had diaper changes.
	     a.m. _____
	     p.m. _____
	     a.m. _____
	     p.m. _____

Daily Update

Child's Name _____

Date _____

A NOTE FROM FAMILY MEMBERS		
Today you can reach me:	◯ at the usual number	◯ at this number
Last night my child slept:	◯ very well ◯ well	◯ less than usual ◯ more than usual

So far my child's mood has been:		
The last feeding was at:		
Special instructions or things to be aware of today include:		
My child will be picked up at:	◯ the usual time	◯ by

A NOTE FROM CAREGIVERS		
Today your child was feeling:		
Your baby enjoyed:		
At lunch your child ate:	◯ everything ◯ some things	◯ most things ◯ very little
Snacks today were:	given at given at	
Just to let you know:		
Naps	Bottles	Diaperings

Chapter 2: Creating Your Environment

The environment of a quality infant program is more than the arrangement of furniture and the selection of toys. A quality environment encourages family involvement. It ensures that infants are safe and that their development is encouraged, and makes it easy for caregivers to spend quality time with individual children. It is the visual expression of all that your program stands for.

Space Requirements

People often think that because infants are small, they do not need much space. This is not true! Baby items take up a lot of space. Remember, you need room for cribs, changing tables, and other baby equipment. Most states require a higher child-to-caregiver ratio for infants, so you need room for several adults. Mobile babies need space to explore, and because most infants see other babies as nothing more than interesting objects to poke, grab, and climb upon, you need enough space to be able to keep non-mobile infants safe and mobile infants safely apart from one another. Having enough space, and more important, having well-planned space is crucial to a quality infant program.

Place-Based Program

Basing your program on the physical learning environment is a wonderful way to meet individual children's needs on their own schedules. It means that caregivers carefully plan the furniture, arrangement of space, available toys, and materials so that infants learn as they interact with their surroundings. This enables babies to develop skills and have new experiences at a natural pace as they make their way through the day.

In this type of program, the focus is on each individual child. All infants in a room are rarely doing the same thing at the same time. Instead caregivers are able to meet the unique needs of each individual child by setting out materials that fit each infant's developmental stage. Much time is spent getting to know and understand individual infants so that their needs can be anticipated and met. While special activities are often a planned part of the day, they do not take place at a specific "activity time." Instead they can occur at any time throughout the day.

Because your space is your primary teaching tool, it is important that your infant room is a comfortable, familiar place for all of your babies and their families. Learn about the cultural backgrounds of the infants in your care, and be as culturally diverse and inclusive in the materials, furniture, pictures, books, and music that you provide. This will help all infants to thrive in your program.

Learning environments should do the following:
✿ Promote all areas of development (language, sensory, social, emotional, cognitive, and motor)
✿ Encourage a positive self-concept and support home cultures
✿ Encourage positive social interactions
✿ Promote diversity and avoid racial or sex-role stereotypes

Entrance

The entrance is your program's first impression. It is the first thing that families see and the one area of your program that family members will enter every day. As a result, this space should be family friendly. Consider displaying in this space photos of the children engaged in activities both at your program and with their families. This sends the message that you not only value a child's daily experiences but that you value her family as well.

The entrance is also a great place to encourage communication with families. Hang a clipboard for each child at eye level where family members can review their child's daily chart. If wall space is an issue, consider a box of hanging files, one per child, where families can find daily charts and other communications such as newsletters or parenting information.

Your entrance is also likely to be the site of many hellos and goodbyes. If your space is large enough, you may want to include a comfortable chair or two where family members can sit with their child to say goodbye or take a moment to snuggle before heading back home at the end of the day. Cubbies for children's personal items and a counter or bench where family members can dress and undress infants are also useful.

Indoor Spaces

In addition to the entrance, several other indoor spaces will make up your infant program. These spaces include a food-preparation and eating area, a sleeping area, a diapering area, and exploration and play areas including active play and quiet play. These areas may be defined by pre-existing walls or by the arrangement of low shelves or other furniture. Lofts at a height appropriate for infants are another great way to define an area. Not only do they provide a separate, secluded space, but they give children a new vantage point from which to view the room as well. A loft can also provide valuable storage underneath. No matter what you use to define and separate spaces, make sure that infants can be easily observed by their caregivers. You will also

CREATING YOUR ENVIRONMENT

want to be sure that the layout of the furniture allows both infants and caregivers to move easily from space to space. As you are defining your areas, here are some tips to consider:

- Set up your space to require few rules: Make off-limits areas inaccessible to infants, and make sure that everything in infant areas is touchable and mouthable.
- Avoid overstimulation: Limit the number of objects in and around cribs or changing tables, and be selective about toys in play areas.
- Think about how space affects behavior: Large, open areas encourage active exploration and crawling. Small spaces encourage concentration and social interaction.
- Think about maintenance: Make sure the floor under eating and other messy areas can be easily cleaned and that the surfaces that children will crawl upon are soft and also easily cleaned. Be consistent about where you store items, and organize and label storage space.
- Think about staff comfort: Provide comfortable seating with back support for adults as they sit with infants, and make sure that cribs and changing tables are at a comfortable height.

Both our behaviors and our moods can be greatly influenced by our physical environments, so it is important that the space you create is visually pleasing to both caregivers and infants. Display pictures at child height. A low fish tank with a secured lid can be both soothing and entertaining to young children. No matter how you fill your space, remember, too much stimulation can be overwhelming and makes infants passive observers who demand entertainment rather than active participants who are able to keep themselves busy.

Meeting Needs

Food Area

Whether your food area includes a complete kitchen or simply a bottle warmer and a sink and small fridge, make sure you have space for high chairs, tables, and chairs with infant seats, and possibly a comfortable chair for adults to sit in and feed babies. You will also want to have plenty of bottles and child-size utensils handy. Keep this area organized by including ample storage and by labeling items. Space to store and label baby food

and formula is especially important if you are asking family members to bring these items from home.

Sleeping Area

The sleeping area should be in the quietest spot possible. Here, arrange cribs, bassinets, and cradles far enough apart so that infants will not disturb one another. Include mobiles or other items for babies to look at. These items should be for self-soothing. Avoid using the crib as a playpen. Infants should only be in their cribs when they are sleeping or preparing to sleep. Cribs limit infant mobility and are not conducive to social interaction and bonding. Also, if babies only use cribs for sleeping, they learn to associate cribs with the act of sleeping and are more likely to sleep in them. To accommodate adults, the sleeping area should include rockers or other comfortable chairs for cuddling with children.

Diapering Area

Make sure this area is near a sink or bathroom. Here organization is critical. Keep important items within easy reach for caregivers who are likely to be handling squirming infants. You might want to include a large, wall-mounted mirror positioned for babies to look into, and you may wish to have an easy-to-clean toy handy. Keep in mind, diapering is an excellent opportunity for caregivers to give infants quality one-on-one time, so avoid overstimulating babies with too many visual distractions and toys. Be sure to have close by a covered diaper pail, hand sanitizer, and a spray bottle that contains a disinfecting solution.

Indoor Exploration and Play Space

Much of your space will be dedicated to encouraging infants to play and explore. While in your program infants need an opportunity to be active and loud. They also need to be able to escape from the noise and activity and have opportunities to engage in quiet play. Your indoor space will need to accommodate all of these needs. One effective way to ensure that infants have the opportunity to explore and engage all areas of development as they play in your space is through the creation of exploration centers.

Exploration Centers

Many preschool programs divide their space into distinct activity areas or learning centers. While the focus of these centers may be different for infants, this basic concept also works well with older infants. Here are some advantages of learning centers:

- Materials are more likely to be found, used, and put away because they are kept in or near the area where they will most likely be used.
- Children are more likely to spread out as they take advantage of different centers of interest.
- Children are able to see a variety of new activities or experiences they can choose to engage in.
- Children are more likely to stay focused on an activity of their choosing.

When using the learning center concept with older infants, the specific exploration centers you choose to provide should be designed to encourage the exploration of specific skills or areas of development. For example, you could have a gross motor center, where children can climb, crawl, step, and slide. In a sensory center children can explore different textures or smells, discover mirrors, and play with musical instruments.

When working with infants, especially if you have a variety of ages in your group, you may want to set up only one exploration center and change its focus based on the children's developmental needs or interests. No matter how many centers you choose to set up, the location is important and deserves careful thought. A gross motor center will need a lot of space, while a book nook should be in a small, quiet area. If you set these two centers next to each other, your quiet space is not going to be very successful. Some centers can go anywhere; others have specific needs. For example, an art center should be near a sink and over a floor surface that can be washed easily. Once you have an idea of the centers you would like to provide and where each will go, use low shelves, climbing structures, and other furniture to define and separate each space.

With your exploration centers in place, the next step is deciding which materials to set out. The amount of materials you make available will depend on the size of the center and the available child-accessible storage. Young children can become overwhelmed by too many choices, so be selective about what you set out. Observe the children carefully as they explore each center, and pay attention to which items they choose. If something is not being used, remove it and replace it with something else. You can also change up the centers based on themes or areas of interest. One week a sensory center may be full of bubble wrap, crinkled craft paper, and other textured materials. The next week you can put those materials away and set out scoops and a bin of coffee grounds mixed with sand. Inevitably, different children will choose to play with and explore different materials, depending on their interests and abilities.

Learning center areas to consider for infants:
✿ Wet or Messy: for art and sensory experiences
✿ Reaching, Grasping, and Kicking: balls, rattles, and activity gyms
✿ Language and Book: posters, board books, pictures
✿ Climbing: sturdy items to climb over, under, and through
✿ Mirror: low, shatterproof mirrors to explore
✿ Blocks: large, soft blocks and smaller blocks for filling and dumping
✿ Soft Toy and Cozy: nook filled with pillows, stuffed animals, and other soft toys
✿ Costume: hats, feather boas, and other items with different textures to explore
✿ Action and Reaction: busy boxes, sorting boxes, pounding toys, and other activities
✿ Sound: tape recorders, instruments, and other sound-making toys to explore
✿ Animals: live animals, stuffed animals, plastic animals, and pictures of animals

Even in the most well-thought-out learning center environment, materials are likely to wander. Carrying things from place to place is just what infants love to do! When children are finished using items, encourage them to put the items away, but avoid controlling children's movement. Positive experiences should be encouraged wherever they spontaneously occur. Be flexible and have realistic expectations of the infants in your care.

Active Play

Your indoor active play area should include a variety of surfaces and spaces to explore. Choice is important, even for infants, so provide a variety of toys on low, sturdy shelves or in open bins that they can access easily. Be conscious of the amount of toys you set out. Too many toys can be overwhelming, and too much clutter can inhibit movement. To an active infant, a bin full of toys is an invitation to play fill-and-dump games. Instead, select a few toys, and put them out on open shelves that infants can easily access. If you have a lot of toys, consider rotating them, but keep a few favorites. You will see the children's excitement when they discover new toys.

Use mats and firm pillows to create protected areas where less-mobile infants can practice gross motor skills, such as rolling over and scooting, without the worry of foot traffic. Make sure that this area is large enough to allow babies to really move. Ideally it should be large enough to allow a caregiver to be in the space with her infants as well.

More-mobile infants need opportunities to crawl, climb, and pull up. Use a few thick mats stacked to create low, climbable surfaces. Carpet-covered low steps or platforms also work well. These infants will use low tables, bookshelves, or any other nearby furniture to pull up on. Make sure that

Toys to promote gross motor skills	
push-pull toys	tumbling mats
riding toys	balls
tunnels	climbers and slides
large cardboard boxes	vinyl-covered foam
wagons	furniture
Toys to promote fine motor skills	
rattles	knob puzzles (1–3 pieces)
soft balls	containers to dump and fill
busy boxes	shape sorters
stacking rings	

everything in this area is sturdy and will not topple. Mobile infants love their new ability to move around and explore. Support this exciting stage of development by providing them with both hard and soft surfaces to crawl across. Lay some linoleum on top of carpet, or a rug over a hardwood floor.

Quiet Play

Your quiet play space should have a calm and soothing atmosphere. Have plenty of cushions and comfortable places for both adults and infants to sit, snuggle, and read. Consider playing soft, soothing music to calm children. Here you can make available grasping toys, puzzles with large knobs, and other quiet activities. Infants can also enjoy quiet time on walks in backpacks or in strollers, but beware of restricting infants' movements too often. To encourage development, they should spend the majority of their waking time in nonrestrictive settings rather than in cribs, highchairs, infant seats, or other situations where they cannot move freely.

Although it is not considered quiet play, think about offering a family-friendly private space where mothers can comfortably nurse their babies. This is a subtle way to support families and can be helpful for transitioning young infants into and out of your program each day.

Outdoor Spaces

Taking infants outdoors does require a little extra planning, but it is well worth the effort. All children, including infants, should spend some active time outdoors. It is good for their health and emotional well-being. When taking infants outside, consider a few aspects. Be sure to have an easy and safe way to transport babies. One caregiver will not be able to carry three infants in her arms. Once infants are outside, you will need a safe place on the ground to place them. Taking an infant outdoors but leaving her in a stroller or bouncy chair restricts her movement and prevents her from interacting with the natural world.

Young infants will need a soft, enclosed space where they can lie, roll, and kick without being stepped on. You can use blankets, mats, or even soft grass. Use vinyl-covered foam or other objects, such as well-placed benches or strollers with the wheels locked, to create a semiprotected space. If you use benches or strollers, be sure they will not topple. Check the ground around your outdoor infant area carefully to ensure that it is free of things that may be harmful, such as glass, nails, litter, and so on. Make sure this area is in the shade, as infants'

skin is very sensitive to the sun. Babies will enjoy viewing other children playing. Elevated infant swings allow babies to take in the sights and use some different muscles. Finally, be sure to have some comfortable seating for caregivers as well.

Older mobile infants love cruising and exploring the outdoors. For them, include safe places to crawl and climb. Logs, tree stumps, and even old tires (after careful inspection) are great objects for them to pull up on, crawl over, and straddle. Infant or seat swings are always an exciting experience. Sandboxes provide an interesting texture to explore, and leaves and sticks are very engaging to the senses. These children are also sun sensitive, so be sure to have ample shade in your outdoor area or otherwise protect the infants. Mobile infants need to be watched carefully as they move about outdoors, because many still use their mouths as an important tool for discovering and exploring new objects. While outdoor time may keep you on your toes, it is well worth the effort. Opportunities to make discoveries in nature are very beneficial to a young child's body and mind.

Chapter 3: Planning Your Program

Program planning includes all of the elements of your program that are not related to your room and furniture. When planning your infant program remember this: *Child care environments are not schools; they are places to live.*

Good homes are the best models for infant and toddler care. Good homes give children a sense of belonging. Learning experiences occur every day as infants move about and explore or watch older children and other family members. Time is basically unscheduled. Events and activities are constantly popping up, but in a natural way. If a baby seems tired, the family is likely to put off that morning trip to the grocery store that had been planned. Families make adjustments to fit the baby's internal schedule, and not the other way around. Also, inside the home, family members have taken the time to childproof everything, and this allows mobile infants to explore freely. Children are being watched, but they have the freedom to move about on their own terms and find quiet places to be by themselves if they feel the need. In general, a good home is a place where young children feel supported, safe, carefree, and unscheduled.

Grouping Infants

Infants are unique little beings, completely absorbed in their own sensory and motor development, and focused on creating a bond with the person who cares for them. They are not developmentally ready to be in large groups. Below are the recommended minimum child-to-caregiver ratio guidelines required for accreditation by the National Association for the Education of Young Children (NAEYC, 2007).

Age	Group size: 6	Group size: 8	Group size: 10	Group size: 12
Birth to 15 months	1:3	1:4	x	x
12–28 months	1:3	1:4	1:4	1:4

These ratios were developed for NAEYC program accreditation and are helpful guides, but they do not represent a national standard. It is important that you check on the legal requirements of your state before grouping children.

We discussed this chart earlier as we explored the importance of helping infants and their caregivers bond, and it is also a useful guide as you explore your options for grouping children. The decision to use a primary caregiver system is a separate issue from how you group the infants, because it can work with any grouping style.

As important as a good child-to-caregiver ratio may be, it is not the only consideration when deciding how to group the infants in your program. Their ages, developmental stages, and needs are also important, as are the interests and skills of your staff. Your program space will also impact grouping. You may legally be able to put 10 mobile infants in a room with three staff, but if your space is broken up into very small rooms, you might want to consider creating smaller groups. There are many ways to group young children, including mixed-age grouping, same-age grouping, and flexible-age grouping.

Mixed-Age Grouping

Mixed-age grouping is how children are naturally grouped in families and has many advantages. It can be less stressful for children than same-age grouping because it honors their individual differences. Caregivers naturally expect children of different ages to have different abilities and interests. While we all know this to be true, in single-age grouping there is a strong temptation to compare children and to have all children doing the same thing at the same time. The temptation to put all children on the same schedule is also reduced in mixed-age groupings, making it easier to honor each individual infant's internal clock.

In mixed-age groups, older children interact with younger children, playing, helping, and watching one another. Being more skilled and independent than the others in their group boosts older children's confidence. Younger children also benefit. They learn new skills and are motivated to try new things by watching and playing with their older friends. Another advantage to mixed-age groups is that siblings can be grouped together. This can be a great benefit for families. Often in mixed-age groupings, the group (caregivers and children) stays the same over a period of years, creating a more stable environment for children.

There are some disadvantages to mixed-age grouping. This approach may be restricted by state guidelines. Caregivers may focus their attention on one particular age or developmental stage. And because some states (and NAEYC accreditation guidelines) require that the child-to-caregiver ratio be in compliance with the age of the youngest member of the group, mixed-age grouping can also be more expensive.

Same-Age Grouping

Same-age grouping has some advantages for staff. It is easier to put children on the same schedule (although this is not always best for the children). It is easier to ensure that all of the materials that children can access are developmentally appropriate. Some caregivers may prefer same-age grouping because they are more comfortable with or are drawn to a particular developmental stage. Family members may be more comfortable with same-age groups, out of concern that older children may harm their infants or that younger children may hinder the development of older children. This is purely an issue of perception.

The primary disadvantage of same-age grouping for children is that they are often removed from a familiar group at a time dictated by the calendar and not based on their needs. When children change groups, their caregiver often changes as well, which can be unsettling for infants and works against caregiver bonding. This can be addressed by having caregivers follow the same group of children up through the years.

Flexible-Age Grouping

Flexible-age grouping combines some of the elements of same-age grouping with mixed-age grouping. Here children are put into groups based on natural developmental breaks. The range of ages is not as wide as with mixed-age grouping, but it is wide enough to allow younger children to learn from older children. This approach is also good for caregivers, because they do not have to manage a full spectrum of developmental abilities, but there is enough variety in developmental stages that children are not competing for the same resources. Many program administrators find this grouping helpful because it reduces the stress both caregivers and children experience when the calendar indicates a child should be moved to the next room but space is not available. One example of flexible-age grouping ranges follows:

- 6 weeks to 15 months (limited language and not walking consistently)
- 12 months to 30 months (developing language and walking)
- 24 months to 36 months (proficient language)

No matter which method of grouping you choose, you can create a more cohesive environment among all of the children and staff if you encourage mixed-age experiences in small groups on a regular basis. These experiences could be at lunchtime, during outdoor play, or for special activities.

Creating a Schedule

When thinking about a daily schedule for infant programs, one golden rule holds true: the younger the child, the more flexible and individualized the schedule needs to be. As a caregiver, you need to provide not only consistency but also more than a touch of flexibility. A predictable schedule will help an infant feel more secure. However, being flexible in that schedule will help you to meet the immediate needs of individual infants, which are sure to arise. Having some flexibility can also help you to take advantage of unplanned learning experiences.

To be flexible and consistent, consider a schedule based on events rather than on time. Individual infants generally come to your program with their own internal or home schedule already set. They wake up, have a diaper change, and eat. They might have a little tummy time, and then it is time for their mid-morning nap. They wake up, have another diaper change, and it is play time, and so on. Remember, your program needs to fit the child, not the other way around. Learn as much as you can about each infant's home schedule and internal rhythms, and try to keep to them. Individual infant schedules are also important to consider when assigning infants to a primary caregiver. Consider the following basic care elements when planning your daily schedule:

- Arrivals and departures
- Feeding and food preparation (meals and snacks)
- Diapering
- Sleeping
- Dressing

Aside from meeting an infant's basic needs, a daily schedule should also include the following:

- Active play time and quiet, cuddling times
- Time with others, time alone, and one-on-one time
- Child-chosen activities and those offered by adults
- Indoor and outdoor play experiences

Here is a sample infant schedule for a full-day program:

- Arrival and undressing (outerwear)
- Welcome with cuddling and independent explorations
- Outdoor time
- Lunch
- Quiet time
- Outdoor time
- Independent explorations
- Prepping for goodbye

Notice, there are no times posted on this schedule. If several children are struggling with separation issues, the "welcome" block will take more time than it might on days when most of the infants transition easily into your program. If the infants are fussy or you need a change of scenery, shorten your time indoors and head outside. You may also notice that diapering, feedings and snacks, and naps are not included in this schedule. Infants have their own internal clocks that regulate these events. Different children will need these basic-care needs addressed at different times. Fortunately, individuals are pretty predictable. Once you know when each infant in your care needs a nap or a bottle, you can work those needs into your schedule.

One of the joys of being an infant caregiver is watching and being a part of the new discoveries children make every day. Enjoy the infants' experiences as they explore the environment you have created for them. Do not rush them on to the next activity. Infants are not thinking about what is going to happen next; they are focused on the "now." If you have developed a thoughtful schedule and have planned ahead, you will be able to enjoy the "now," too.

Planning

The daily schedule is the skeleton of your program. Planning is what fleshes it out. Planning ahead, short-term and long-term, will help you to be sure that you are meeting the needs of each child. Taking the time to plan ahead will also ensure that you are providing many varied and enriching experiences for the infants in your care. Current brain research shows that early experiences help to form important pathways in infants' brains, laying the foundation for future learning.

Like every other aspect of your infant program, planning here is very different from planning for other ages. For infants you will think about providing experiences, which are open ended, more than activities that have one desired outcome. To do this successfully, a lot of thought should be put into elements in your space. For example, you may decide that a few of the infants need more sensory experiences. Caregivers accustomed to planning for older children might consider gathering a group around the sensory table to touch different fabric squares. If you try this with infants, a few may be interested and touch or mouth a few of the squares, then move on. Others will have no interest and will try to wander away or will become fussy because you are keeping them from exploring other areas of the room. Some may even protest strongly and leave you trying to manage a meltdown while trying to supervise the texture activity at the same time.

You and the infants in your care will benefit more if you think about how you can add a new element to your physical space that will give them the opportunity to explore different textures if they choose to. You could add a variety of different carpet squares and rubber mats to the play area. Exploring these items is an experience that does not have to be closely supervised or managed by you. Instead, those infants who are interested will spend a lot of time exploring these new elements. Some will be fascinated by the variety of textures and will explore them with their hands or by crawling across them. Other infants might try to pick them up, flip them over, push them around, or pile them up. Different children will be engaged with the materials for different reasons, depending on their developmental interests. This is what makes the experience open ended. With these experiences, you are then able to spend time with the children, enjoying their new discoveries and keeping track of their development.

Finger paints and other art materials can also provide enriching sensory experiences for older infants. These children will get a lot out of simply feeling the paint on their fingers and moving the paint across the paper. When doing art projects with infants, remember that they are focused on the process, not the product. The experience will be much more enjoyable for you and the child if you enter it with the understanding that things will get messy as infants dive in to these wonderful sensory-rich materials, and the end result may not look like much. Many children will not pay attention to what they are making until they are three years old, so avoid craft activities that ask infants to create a specific finished product.

Important Program Goals and Objectives for Infants:
✦ To feel valued, competent, and supported
✦ To express feelings appropriately
✦ To develop positive relationships with adults and peers
✦ To learn to communicate (verbally and nonverbally
✦ To develop motor and self-help skills
✦ To develop thinking skills
✦ To experience consistency between home and caregiver environments

All successful planning relies on two things: observation and evaluation. Watch the infants in your care carefully. Where are they each developmentally? What are their likes and dislikes? When are they more apt to be open to new experiences, and when are they fussier?

Next, take a look at your program's general goals and objectives. Are you doing enough to support these goals? Keeping daily anecdotal records (notes describing each child, what she is doing, how she reacts to a situation) can be very helpful here. Taking time each day to write about a child (even if it is just one sentence) will give you great insight into behavior patterns and that particular child's experience in your program. All you have to do is look back over your notes, and the answers to these important planning questions should be there. Once these questions are answered, making individual goals should be easy.

When you have an idea of what you would like to do, write it down. Make a note of the goals and objectives you have for each child. Goals are more long-term, and objectives are the small steps you need to take to reach those goals. Create a to-do list, including materials you will need and any changes you will need to make to your environment. The more you have done ahead of time, the more smoothly the activities will go and the more time you will have to enjoy the experiences. Most important, be flexible. You may be excited to introduce them to soap bubbles, but if the day comes and several of the babies are fussy or not feeling well, the experience will probably be more successful if you wait for another day. Children's moods are not the only variables that might cause you to alter your plans. Consider unexpected events and your own mood as well.

Exposure to language is important for infants. Long before they are able to speak, infants are learning about conversational rhythms, that words come from sounds and have meaning, and that words communicate ideas. For this reason, as you are planning, it is important to think about how you are going to provide rich language experiences every day for the infants in your care. This can be done in many ways.

- **Reading books:** When you read with infants, you are introducing new sounds, words, and ideas that build vocabulary. You are also introducing basic concepts of print such as how to hold a book, turn pages, and the very basic idea that books communicate stories or information.

- **Storytelling:** Making up stories and talking to infants develops listening skills and promotes language development and emotional bonding. Storytelling is especially good for personalizing the language experience. You can adjust the length and complexity of the story based on the development of the individual child, and you can make the stories personally relevant to children, helping to develop language and vocabulary that relates to their life experiences and cultural background.

- **Songs and rhymes:** Traditional songs, nursery rhymes, and silly songs and rhymes that you create all help children to understand that words are created by putting together different sounds. This sound (or phonemic) awareness is the foundation for speech and later for reading.

It is important to plan for daily opportunities for infants to engage in these experiences. When you read, tell stories or sing songs with infants, keep in mind that every child is different and there is no "right way" for a child to listen to or engage in the experiences you provide. Some infants may sit happily in your lap, pointing to the items pictured as you flip through the pages of a board book, or watch you attentively as you sing a song. Other children may sit for a moment but then will wiggle and crawl around. Adjust the experience to fit the needs of the child. Instead of reading the entire book, consider flipping through the pages. Talk about the pictures that are interesting to the child or simply let the child flip pages. This experience alone is building important fine motor skills and promoting book awareness. You might even close the book and change the language experience. Sing a song or talk with the child about whatever it is they choose to engage in next. Alternatively you could continue reading for a few moments longer to see if another child might wander over to listen. Your role is to provide infants with rich language experiences, and then follow their lead as they engage in those experiences.

Evaluating

At the end of the day, evaluate. Did you do the special activities you had planned? Did you meet any goals or objectives? If not, why not? Maybe the activities, or even the goals themselves, were inappropriate, or perhaps something unexpected happened. Could you do anything differently next time to make the experience better? If things went even better than expected, try to figure out why. Do not limit your evaluations to the special activities that you plan. Babies grow and change quickly. A good infant program should constantly evaluate the following:

- ✿ Changes to the environment
- ✿ Changes to the daily routine
- ✿ Program goals and objectives
- ✿ Individual infant goals and objectives
- ✿ Family involvement
- ✿ Special activities and experiences

Even infant behavior can help you to evaluate your program. Much of the "bad" behavior that infants exhibit can be prevented by making changes to your program. If you are having behavior problems in your infant group, evaluate the following:

- ✿ Expectations: Are they realistic?
- ✿ Materials: Are there too few or too many?
- ✿ Children's experiences: Are they bored, frustrated, or overwhelmed?
- ✿ Space: Is it too crowded or too open?
- ✿ Scheduling: Are children required to wait or sit still too much? Is the schedule chaotic or unpredictable? Is it conflicting with infants' internal clocks?
- ✿ Temptations: Are forbidden areas too easy to get to?
- ✿ Noise: Is the environment too noisy or overstimulating?

Here is a form to help you in your planning and evaluating.

Weekly Planning Form

Week of _____

Experiences and skills to emphasize _____

Changes to the environment

Special activities to offer this week

	Monday	Tuesday	Wednesday	Thursday	Friday
Songs Stories Games					
Indoor Exploration					
Outdoor Exploration					

Changes to daily routines

Involving families

My to-do list

Chapter 4: Assessment

You have your program up and running. Your environment and schedule have been carefully thought out, and you have taken the time to select experiential activities for your group of infants. But how do you know if you are being effective?

It is time to think about how to evaluate each child's progress. Assessments are the final component to a successful program. By documenting the infants' progress in an organized and consistent way, you will not only learn about where each child is developmentally throughout the year, you will also gain valuable information about how successfully your program is meeting the needs of the children. Armed with this information, you can modify the experiences, curriculum, or physical environment to grow and improve your overall program.

Authentic Assessment Practices

A multiple-choice exam taken on a particular day often does not show a person's true knowledge or abilities. Young children are even more sensitive to pressure or "forced" situations. Often, infants will not perform for you at all. To get a clear picture of a child's abilities, any assessments you do should include the following aspects:

- Be ongoing: To truly get a handle on children's progress, assessments should be done several times throughout the year. As you look back over previous assessments, evidence of a child's growth (or lack of growth) will be clear.

- Be closely related to your daily program or curriculum: Bringing in an assessment tool that is very different from the routine of your regular program can be unsettling to children and, therefore, may not be a true measure of what they are capable of.

- Be used in a child's natural play environment: Children are more likely to experiment with emerging skills when they are in comfortable, familiar situations. A natural play environment will give you a more accurate measure of the skills a child is working on.

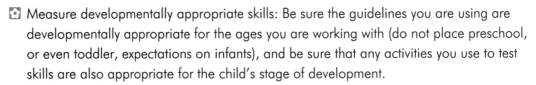

- Measure developmentally appropriate skills: Be sure the guidelines you are using are developmentally appropriate for the ages you are working with (do not place preschool, or even toddler, expectations on infants), and be sure that any activities you use to test skills are also appropriate for the child's stage of development.

- Cover all relevant domains, and account for different learning styles: Remember children develop holistically, meaning that as their motor skills develop, so do their language skills. As their language skills develop, so do their social skills, and so forth. While we may think of each area of developmental individually, all areas are actually quite interconnected. Be sure you choose a variety of activities to ensure you are accurately measuring progress in all areas of development.

- Include the family as an important source of information: Families are partners in their children's education. The more information you can get about a child's family and home situation, the more complete a picture you will have of that child and the more accurately you can interpret assessment results.

Some Assessment Options

The more methods you use to measure a child's progress, the more accurate a picture you will get. Of course, you want any method you use to be in line with the authentic assessment practices mentioned above. Two methods that work especially well with young children are the individual portfolio and planned activity assessments using an assessment instrument (rubric or chart).

The Individual Portfolio

An individual portfolio is a file or three-ring binder where you keep samples of a child's work or evidence of an infant's development that you have collected throughout the year. This method has the advantage of working seamlessly with your everyday routine and activities, and can show very clearly how a child is progressing over time.

You can use photos, observations and anecdotal records, samples of a child's work, notes from family members, videos, and so on as entries in a portfolio. When working with infants, you are less likely to be collecting work samples and more likely to be using other documentation tools such as photos and observations. Portfolios should include a record of typical skills and experiences for a child at different points in the year as well as important "firsts" (the first time he used a word to communicate or he climbed up a step). With so many possibilities, creating a good portfolio can be an overwhelming challenge. Here are some tips to keep you organized and focused.

- ◘ For each child, use a three-ring binder containing clear sleeves for storing photographs, work samples, or notes.

- ◘ Use dividers to create distinct assessment areas that make sense for your program, for example motor, language, social and emotional, cognitive, and so on. It is inevitable that some of the evidence you collect will fit into more than one category. This is why it is important that you think about the reason you are choosing to include each portfolio entry.

- ◘ Plan in advance. Think about the skills you want to track, the "firsts" you want to collect, and how you want to show evidence of progress. Make the decision to gather specific work samples or other evidence at specific points in the year. This does not mean that on the first Tuesday in October you will take a finger painting sample from everyone. You want to make sure that the samples you select represent what is typical for that child. If he is having unusual difficulty or showing a lack of interest in the activity that day, wait until you have a more typical sample to enter.

- ◘ Use your state's standards, curriculum guidelines, or the developmental milestones included in this book to guide your planning. This way, your program will be able to show clear evidence of working toward those goals.

- ◘ Be selective about the work you save. Include evidence of important developmental milestones (a photo of a child attempting to crawl taken at the beginning of the year, a photo of the first time a child crawls, another photo or video clip and description of the child crawling later in the year). But also include individualized items that showcase a child's unique skills or interests.

- ◘ Document your reasons for saving the work. Use the forms included in this book, or create your own method for explaining each entry. Just be sure that each entry is dated and includes an explanation of what skill it is intending to showcase.

Sample Portfolio Entry Form

Use the following form to describe each portfolio piece you collect. Simply fasten it to the work collected or slide it into a clear sheet protector along with the work sample. As you look back over the portfolio, these forms will help you to identify the purpose of each piece in the collection.

```
                    Portfolio Piece

Child's Name: Parker                    Date: 1/17/11

Activity: Roller Painting               Collected by: Susan

┌──────────────────────────────────────────────────────┐
│ Skill(s) displayed:                                    │
│   Rotates wrist to manipulate objects                  │
│                                                        │
│ Comments:                                              │
│   Parker worked hard to get the ball to move all over  │
│   the paper                                            │
└──────────────────────────────────────────────────────┘
```

Planned Activity Assessments

During planned activity assessments, teachers use an assessment instrument, such as a chart or rubric, to track evidence of the skills a child demonstrates during a particular planned activity. Children participate in the planned activity just as they usually would with any program activity or experience. The only difference is that caregivers make note of the skills they see infants demonstrate as they play or explore. The activity and recording chart are carefully planned and prepared in advance. The pre-arranged experiences and caregiver observations typically go on over a period of time, usually several weeks, to make sure that every child has been observed doing behavior that is typical for that child. The assessment is then repeated again later in the year. Planned activity assessments allow teachers to clearly see the skills that each child in their program is demonstrating at a particular point in time. This type of assessment is a great way to get a baseline measure of a child's abilities, and when repeated again later in the year, evidence of progress (or lack of progress) is very clear. While it may seem much simpler than maintaining individual portfolios, planned activity assessments require a lot of thought and staff time. Here are some tips to make them successful:

- Make sure assessed activities or experiences are natural play situations for the children. Children will only show their true skills if they feel comfortable.

- Be clear about the skills you are looking for, and prepare a recording chart in advance. An example of a recording chart is included in this book.

- Select a few high-interest activities that lend themselves to assessing a variety of skills. You want to be sure the experiences you choose will engage a variety of children with different interests and skills. Many of the activities in this book make great planned assessment activities.

- Set up several planned activity stations with a staff person assigned to each. Be sure you have enough staff or additional adult support on hand to encourage children not engaged in the targeted activities to become involved, or else make sure these children are adequately supervised.

- Allow plenty of time, up to six weeks, to complete assessments on all children. The first assessment period always takes the longest. Once caregivers are familiar with the children, the assessment procedure, and the activities, later assessments will go much more smoothly.

- After the assessment is over, be prepared to shadow those children who you feel did not show their true skills. Make notes of the skills you see in their everyday play. You want to be sure you get an accurate read on every child's abilities.

- Plan to complete assessments on all children at least twice a year to show progress.

Sample Assessment Instrument

Use the following form to help you identify the skills children demonstrate while you observe an assessment activity. Note any modifications you make. By using one form per child and by using the same form again later in the year, evidence of progress and development will be very clear.

The Family Component

Families are the best source of information about the infants in your care. Be sure to include them in the assessment process. At the beginning of each school year, encourage families to fill out a simple form that will help you to get to know their children, as well as the families' routines, goals, and concerns. We have included a sample form in this book. Whether you use it as part of an initial home visit or include it among the required paperwork to enroll a child in your program, it will send a clear message to family members that they play an important role in your program and that their voices will be heard.

Continuing to keep the lines of communication with families open throughout the year is also important. Many children behave quite differently at school than they do at home; so, the picture of a child's developmental progress may be incomplete without some idea of the skills he may be demonstrating at home. One way to consistently communicate with families is to pass a journal back and forth from home to school. This weekly informal correspondence allows teachers and family members to share anecdotes about the children along with

Assessment Instrument

12 to 24 months

Activity: Visiting Vehicles
modification: used ball instead of car

Child's Name: Claudia

Observer: Erin

Key:
2- skill mastery
1- skill emerging
0- Not showing interest yet

	Milestone/Standard	Notes	Dates of Assessments 10/11		
Social/ Emotional	Expresses individuality- may insist on doing things, says "no" frequently		not observed		
	Expresses strong feelings and frustration		not observed		
	Seeks approval of parents/caregivers, may be clingy	10/11- looked to me after each roll	1		
	Enjoys the company of peers	10/11- laughed with others	2		
	Models adult behavior		1		
	Identifies one or more body parts		n/o		
	Sensitive to the reactions of others	10/11- visibly upset when Alia threw the ball	1		
	Able to follow clear, simple rules		2		
	Begins to control feelings and use words to express them		1		
	Showing awareness of the feelings of others		1		
	Begins using names for self and others		1		

information about how the children are spending their time in your program and at home. It is also a great way for families and teachers to share any questions or concerns. Specific journal entries can be used as anecdotal evidence of progress in a portfolio. Of course, sensitive issues should be addressed face-to-face and not in a journal.

Regular family member–teacher conferences are another great way to keep the lines of communication open. These can take place at your program or at the child's home. When you are scheduling conferences, make an effort to accommodate a variety of family work schedules. Be flexible and offer choices. Because these meetings are private and face-to-face, they provide a great opportunity to share your concerns about a child, and they give families a chance to bring up their own issues or ask you questions. While a family member–teacher conference does not have to be formal, it is important that you come prepared with specific information about each child's progress. Take notes at these meetings, and review your notes with the families before the meeting is over to make sure you have accurately described any questions, issues, or concerns.

Simple informal conversations at pickup and drop-off times are also a wonderful way to promote communication with family members, although these quick conversations are more difficult to document.

Finally, once you have completed your assessments (or periodically throughout the year, if you are using individual portfolios), take the time to review the information you have collected on individual children with their families to get their input. Many developmental or health issues are first noticed when infants do not follow the typical path through developmental milestones. If you notice any deviations or have concerns with how a child is developing, these concerns should be shared with families. A regularly scheduled review period offers a great opportunity to voice your observations and concerns. The best forum for such a review is a family member–teacher conference as described above.

Creating an Assessment Plan

Planning is a critical component of successful assessments. Take the time to think about your program (staff availability, state mandates, program goals) and what you are trying to learn or gain by doing assessments. This information will help you to choose the type of assessment method or methods that best meet your needs.

Once you know why and how you are doing assessments, it is time to select the activities that will best give the infants the opportunity to demonstrate the skills you are looking to monitor. The final planning step is to map out your time frame and consider the logistics (staff requirements, materials, space) to get it done.

Steps for Successful Assessments
1. Identify why you are doing assessments or assessment goals (to monitor progress, evaluate a program, or comply with mandates).
2. Identify assessment methods that will achieve these goals.
3. Select curriculum-based activities that will showcase targeted skills.
4. Plan the time frame and logistics.
5. Collect the data
6. Evaluate the data.

A good assessment activity is one that gives children of different learning styles and temperaments the opportunity to demonstrate a variety of skills. Many of the activities you typically do in your program every day are great assessment opportunities. Integrating your assessments into your regular program routine is most comfortable for children and will give you a more accurate read on their skills and abilities.

Great Assessment Opportunities and Some of the Developmental Areas Assessments Showcase
✿ Classroom routines and transitions (social and emotional, listening)
✿ Meals and snack (social and emotional, language, motor)
✿ Songs, fingerplays, and story time (language, listening, motor)
✿ Outdoor play (motor, social and emotional, language, cognitive)
✿ Dramatic play (language, motor, social and emotional, cognitive)
✿ Art experiences and manipulatives (motor, cognitive, language)
✿ Conversations with familiar adults (language, listening, social and emotional, cognitive)

Using the Results

Of course, you want to be sure that you track the progress of individual children as their development is monitored and evaluated throughout the year. This information is useful to help caregivers plan new activities and experiences that will support an infant's development. Sharing this information with families is also beneficial. It allows families to see the value of your program and helps to get a clear picture of their infant's growth and progress.

But the usefulness of this data goes beyond monitoring individual children. Once you have compiled all of that data, take the time to look at the big picture. In addition to informing you about the progress of individual children, your assessment data can provide useful information about your program. Look at the overall skill development of all of the infants in each of the

different developmental areas. This will give you an idea of how well your program is meeting your state's guidelines or your program goals. Is there an area where children are not progressing consistently? Do you notice any common traits among the children who are progressing more slowly? Are they of the same temperament, cultural background, or stage of development? This information could give you valuable insight into your program's strengths and weaknesses. Use it to help you make decisions about professional development, teaching, and the curriculum. When data on individuals is compiled to create a picture of your entire program, authentic assessments can help improve overall program quality.

Sample Basic Assessment Schedule

Month 1
- Send out family questionnaire or conduct home visits
- Plan assessment goals, select initial assessment activities, and prepare forms
- Create a portfolio binder for each child

Month 2
- Review family questionnaires with staff
- Plan and coordinate teacher schedules to perform initial assessments
- Begin collecting portfolio pieces

Month 3
- Perform initial planned activity assessments
- Continue collecting portfolio pieces

Month 4
- Schedule family member–teacher conferences to review initial planned activity assessment results and individual portfolios
- Continue collecting portfolio pieces

Month 5
- Plan and coordinate teacher schedules for midyear planned activity assessments using the same activities and forms as the initial assessments
- Continue collecting portfolio pieces

Month 6
- Perform planned activity assessments
- Continue collecting portfolio pieces

Month 7
- Schedule family member–teacher conferences to review planned activity assessments and individual portfolios
- Continue collecting portfolio pieces

Month 8
- Continue collecting portfolio pieces

Month 9
- Plan and coordinate teacher schedules for end-of-year planned activity assessments using the same activities and forms as the initial assessments
- Continue collecting portfolio pieces

Month 10
- Perform planned activity assessments
- Continue collecting portfolio pieces

Month 11
- Schedule family member–teacher conferences to review planned activity assessment results and individual portfolios
- Continue collecting portfolio pieces

Month 12
- As a staff, review all assessment results and portfolios to assess your overall program quality
- Make plans for program improvements and adjustments

About Me and My Family

Date: _____

Child's Name: _____

Date of Birth: _____

A note to family members: This form will help us get to know your child and your family. Knowing your child's regular routines, likes and dislikes, and your goals for your child will help us to better serve your whole family.

About Me

My personality in general is_____

I was born   ❑ Full-term   ❑ Preterm

When I get sick, it is often because of or accompanied by (please check all that apply):

❑ Ear Infections   ❑ RSV   ❑ Stomachache   ❑ Diarrhea
❑ Seizures   ❑ Asthma   ❑ Urinary Infection   ❑ Headaches   ❑ Cough

When it is time to eat, I like to use (please check all that apply):

❑ A bottle   ❑ My hands   ❑ A spoon   ❑ A fork   ❑ I like to be fed

In general, I like ❑ Most foods   ❑ Some foods   ❑ I'm a picky eater

My potty words are _____ (urination) and _____ (bowel movement).

Where I Live (list residences and typical days at each home)

Whose House   Address   Days of the Week

1 _____

_____

2 _____

_____

3 _____

_____

Who Lives with Me (list names and relationship to child, ages of other children, and do not forget pets!)

House 1: _____

House 2: _____

House 3: _____

On a normal day at home, I...(House 1)
(describe daily routine in detail) _____

_____

_____

_____

On a normal day at home, I...(House 2)
(describe daily routine in detail) _____

_____

_____

_____

On a normal day at home, I...(House 3)
(describe daily routine in detail) _____

_____

_____

_____

ASSESSMENT

My family is excited for me to learn and grow.

A few things they hope I will do this year are _____

_____

_____

A few things I hope I will do this year are _____

_____

_____

Growing up can be hard.

A few things my family is worried about are _____

_____

_____

A few things I'm worried about are _____

_____

_____

A few things I love are_____

_____

_____

A few things I do not like at all are_____

_____

_____

Thank you for taking the time to fill out this form! It will help us to get to know your child and your family.

Assessment Instrument

Birth to 6 months

Activity:

Child's Name: _____

Observer:_____

	Milestone or Standard	Notes	Date	Date	Date
Social and Emotional	Is able to feel calm and relaxed with caregiver				
	Expresses stranger anxiety				
	Is able to self-soothe				
	Sustains eye contact and responds to voices				
	Expresses feelings through facial expressions or vocalizations				
	Shows excitement when familiar adult approaches				
Gross Motor	Controls head				
	Raises upper body with arms when lying on stomach				
	Reaches for nearby objects				
	Kicks and thrusts legs				
	Twists torso				
	Hangs onto feet				
	Rolls over				

Milestone or Standard	Notes	Date	Date	Date
Fine Motor				
Uses fingers to explore surfaces				
Grasps objects				
Releases objects				
Reaches for objects				
Plays with hands and feet				
Language				
Expresses different cries for different moods and needs				
Makes happy sounds				
Turns head to speaker				
Smiles when spoken to				
Quiets at the sound of a familiar voice				
Makes and practices sounds when alone				
Uses sound or speech to get and maintain attention				
Conversational: trades coos, encourages you to repeat an action				
Looks for sounds				
Responds to tone of voice				

Assessment Instrument

6 to 12 months

Activity:

Child's Name: _____

Observer: _____

Key:

3 = Skill Mastery: Demonstrates correctly 90% or more of the time

2 = Skill Practicing: Demonstrates correctly 50% of the time

1 = Skill Emerging: Demonstrates correctly less than 50% of the time

0 = Not showing interest yet

	Milestone or Standard	Notes	Date	Date	Date
Social and Emotional	Self-soothes often				
	Expresses strong feelings and frustration				
	Expresses stranger anxiety				
	Seeks approval of caregiver				
	Enjoys seeing other babies				
	Models adult behavior				
Gross Motor	Scoots				
	Crawls				
	Sits independently				
	Climbs stairs and low furniture				
	Pulls up to standing				
	Takes steps holding onto furniture				
	Stands alone				

Milestone or Standard	Notes	Date	Date	Date
Fine Motor				
Throws objects				
Picks up small objects with thumb and forefinger				
Feeds self with fingers				
Uses forefinger to poke and probe				
Claps				
Puts objects in containers and dumps them out				
Language				
Imitates speech sounds				
Shakes head for *no*				
Babbling includes long and short "word" sounds				
Listens when spoken to				
Recognizes words for common items				

Assessment Instrument

12 to 18 months

Activity:

Child's Name: _____

Observer: _____

Key:

3 = Skill Mastery: Demonstrates correctly 90% or more of the time

2 = Skill Practicing: Demonstrates correctly 50% of the time

1 = Skill Emerging: Demonstrates correctly less than 50% of the time

0 = Not showing interest yet

	Milestone or Standard	Notes	Date	Date	Date
Social and Emotional	Expresses individuality: may insist on doing things, says no frequently				
	Expresses strong feelings and frustration				
	Seeks approval of family members and caregivers, may be clingy				
	Enjoys the company of peers				
	Models adult behavior				
	Able to follow clear, simple rules				
	Sensitive to the reactions of others				
Gross Motor	Walks independently				
	Pulls, pushes, and carries items				
	Squats				
	Walks backward				
	Climbs larger furniture				

Milestone or Standard	Notes	Date	Date	Date
Fine Motor				
Turns pages in a book				
Feeds self with spoon				
Uses a cup				
Stacks objects				
Language				
Says 5–10 words relatively clearly				
Directs the attention of others				
Asks for things by pointing				
Points to objects when asked				
Follows simple commands				
Looks at person speaking				

Assessment Instrument

Activity:

Child's Name: _____

Observer: _____

Key:

3 = Skill Mastery: Demonstrates correctly 90% or more of the time
2 = Skill Practicing: Demonstrates correctly 50% of the time
1 = Skill Emerging: Demonstrates correctly less than 50% of the time
0 = Not showing interest yet

Developmental Area	Milestone or Standard	Age	Age	Age

Portfolio Piece

Child's Name: _____   Date: _____

Activity: _____   Collected by: _____

Skill(s) displayed:

Comments:

Portfolio Piece

Child's Name: _____   Date: _____

Activity: _____   Collected by: _____

Skill(s) displayed:

Comments:

Portfolio Piece

Child's Name: _____   Date: _____

Activity: _____   Collected by: _____

Skill(s) displayed:

Comments:

Chapter 5: Infant Growth and Development

Infants are developing at an incredible rate. It seems as if every day they make new discoveries and learn to do something new. From the day they are born, infants are developing motor skills, learning to communicate and interact with the adults in their lives, experiencing and learning to express their emotions, and developing their senses to explore the world. These areas of development are all interconnected; development in one area will encourage the development of another area. As an infant learns to grasp an object *(motor skill)*, he is now able to put that object in his mouth to feel and taste it *(sensory)*. As the infant's brain processes and organizes these experiences, it is laying the foundation for cognitive skill development.

Developmental milestones are important tools for caregivers. They can help you figure out what to expect from the children in your care and help you identify children who may have special needs. But never forget that they are only a guideline. Children can vary greatly in the ages at which they reach a milestone. What is less likely to vary is the order in which children move through these milestones.

We know every child is different. What we need to remember is that every child will develop at his or her own pace. Do not rush children. Infants want and need to perfect each new skill that they discover. For example, an infant will need to stand and push against the ground or your lap with his legs over and over again to build the muscles he needs to stand on his own and eventually walk. Rather than trying to "walk" a baby who is just starting to try to stand, encourage her attempts at standing. Give her plenty of opportunities to practice. Resist the temptation to "help" babies by forcing them into new skills. For instance, placing a baby in a nest of pillows to "help" her sit up does not encourage her to develop the muscles she needs to sit upright herself, and it deprives her of the opportunity to learn how to get into a sitting position on her own.

Here are brief descriptions of developmental skills typical of infants (birth–18 months) as well as milestone charts divided into the developmental areas of fine motor, gross motor, language, and social and emotional skills.

Developmental Milestones by Age

Birth to Three Months

Newborns are completely dependent on their sensory input and reflexes. At this age babies will turn their heads toward sounds and react to unusual sounds and familiar voices. Their movements are jerky and uncontrolled. They can grasp objects but have little control over releasing them. They may begin to hold their heads up for short periods. Newborns' vision, especially depth perception, is developing. Their eyes follow moving objects and are attracted to faces, contrasting colors, and geometric designs. At this age young infants begin to make different cries to communicate different needs. Some may be able to do some self-soothing. They sleep often.

Three to Six Months

At this age, infants begin to develop eye-hand coordination and have more control over their grasping ability. Gross motor skills are limited to lifting their heads and upper chests, and some may be beginning to roll over. These babies enjoy pushing against the floor when they are held in a standing position. They can express their feelings with different cries, smiles, coos, and laughs and respond well to routine and gentleness. By this age an infant should feel strongly bonded to her family member or guardian. Some infants will actively develop this relationship while others require more perseverance from adults. Their teeth may be appearing; however, they continue to ingest mostly fluids. They need two to three regular nap periods a day.

Six to Nine Months

Babies at this age actively explore objects with their mouths. They enjoy banging objects to create noise and are beginning to understand speech and mimic sounds. It is common that they will notice and stop to inspect small specks and crumbs in their fields of vision. These infants can bring their thumbs and fingers together to grasp objects, and they enjoy dropping or throwing games. Other fine motor skills include beginning to manipulate a cup and to eat finger foods. Gross motor skills include scooting forward by pulling with their arms and pushing with their legs, sitting, and pulling themselves into a standing position. At this age infants communicate by giving nonverbal cues about their states of mind or desires. They might flap their arms when excited or bang their trays when they want more food. They can expresses joy and anger and often develop separation anxiety. These infants respond well to routine and encouragement and continue to need at least two regular naps.

Nine to Twelve Months

These infants are active explorers, touching and grabbing everything. Their vision is well developed, and they hear well and enjoy sounds. Some infants at this age may be able to use a few words (ma-ma, bye-bye, and so on). They are beginning to self-feed finger foods and to chew on crackers. Many can drink from a cup but not independently. Gross motor skills include crawling, walking with support (furniture or someone's hand), turning pages of a book, and carrying objects. These infants continue to use their mouths as tools to explore new objects, and their increased mobility, coordination, and curiosity drives them to pull items out of boxes, cupboards, and off of shelves. They can be moody, affectionate, and possessive and are becoming aware of the emotions of others. Babies at this age need adult recognition and appreciation of their new abilities. They may be afraid of new people and things. Their naps continue to be important, two a day.

12 to 18 Months

These infants are constantly moving about and are familiar with household objects. They are learning to open drawers and doors and to manipulate objects. Many infants at this age use two-word sentences and can verbally communicate wants but still rely heavily on gestures. They are learning to use spoons independently and drink from cups but may spill fluids out the sides. Gross motor skills include crawling backward, walking, beginning to run, climbing stairs and chairs, throwing objects indiscriminately, and learning to help put on and take off clothes. These new skills require

that they be watched closely. Infants at this age like to help others and to imitate adults. They are becoming more independent and separate more easily from their family members or caregivers. At this age they may take only one nap some days but need time to slowly reorient after waking.

Milestones by Area of Development

Social and Emotional Milestones

Age	Skills
Birth–6 months	✿ Able to feel calm and relaxed with family members and caregivers ✿ Self-soothes: may suck on fingers, can wait calmly a few minutes to have needs addressed ✿ Expresses feelings such as pleasure, anger, fear, and sadness, especially to family members and caregivers ✿ Shows excitement when familiar adult approaches ✿ May be afraid of strangers
6–12 months	✿ Self-soothes often ✿ Expresses strong feelings and frustration ✿ Feels deeply connected to family members and caregiver: wants approval, may be clingy ✿ Expresses stranger anxiety ✿ Enjoys seeing other babies ✿ Models behavior after the adults around him
12–18 months	✿ Begins to develop self-image ✿ Expresses individuality: may insist on doing things, may say no or tell you what to do ✿ Sensitive to the reactions of others ✿ Enjoys being with other children but cannot yet share ✿ Able to follow clear, simple rules

Gross Motor Milestones

Age	Gross Motor Skills
Birth–3 months	✿ Tense, jerky movements ✿ Wobbles head from side to side when lying on her back ✿ Begins to hold head up
3–6 months	✿ Raises upper body with arms when lying on stomach ✿ Controls head ✿ Reaches for nearby objects ✿ Kicks and thrusts legs ✿ Twists torso ✿ Hangs onto feet ✿ Rolls over
6–12 months	✿ Scoots ✿ Crawls ✿ Sits independently ✿ Climbs stairs and low furniture ✿ Pulls up on furniture to stand ✿ Takes steps holding onto furniture ✿ Stands alone
12–18 months	✿ Walks independently ✿ Pulls, pushes, and carries items ✿ Squats ✿ Walks backward ✿ Climbs larger furniture

Fine Motor Milestones

Age	Fine Motor Skills
Birth–3 months	✿ Grasps objects ✿ Tight fists become more open and relaxed hands ✿ Uses fingers to explore surfaces
3–6 months	✿ Reaches for dangling objects ✿ Plays with hands and feet ✿ Grasps objects purposefully ✿ Releases objects
6–12 months	✿ Throws objects ✿ Picks up small objects with thumb and forefinger ✿ Feeds self with fingers ✿ Uses forefinger to poke and probe ✿ Claps ✿ Puts objects in containers and dumps them out
12–18 months	✿ Turns pages in a book ✿ Holds a crayon ✿ Feeds self with a spoon ✿ Stacks objects

Language Milestones

Age	Communicating	Listening
Birth–3 months	✿ Has different cries for different needs ✿ Makes random happy sounds ✿ Repeats same sounds	✿ Awakens at loud sounds ✿ Turns head to speaker ✿ Smiles when spoken to ✿ Recognizes familiar voice (when crying, quiets down at the sound of your voice)
3–6 months	✿ Conversational: trades coos with you, may make sound or gesture for you to repeat in play ✿ Makes and practices sounds when alone ✿ Uses sounds or speech to get and keep your attention	✿ Responds to tone of voice ✿ Looks for sounds (ringing, rattling)
6–12 months	✿ Imitates speech sounds ✿ Shakes head for *no* ✿ Babbling includes long and short "word" sounds ✿ Says a few simple words (may not be very clear)	✿ Listens when spoken to ✿ Recognizes words for common items
12–18 months	✿ Says 5–10 words relatively clearly ✿ Directs the attention of others toward things of interest ✿ Asks for things by pointing	✿ Looks at person speaking ✿ Follows simple commands ✿ Points to objects when asked (body parts, pictures of familiar objects in a book)

Working with Infants with Special Needs

Every child is unique and develops differently, but some infants may enter your program with clearly identified special needs. Other children may have developmental issues or special needs identified while in your care. No matter how or when a child is identified as having a special need, it is clear that early intervention and the support of specialists greatly benefits these children and their families.

Understanding the Language of Special Needs

Because it is likely that you will provide care for an infant with an identified or unidentified special need, it is important that you become familiar with some of the language and terms used in the field of special education.

At-Risk: a term used to describe a child who, because of environmental, socioeconomic, family history, or other factors, is considered more likely to develop a temporary or permanent special need. For example, a child who can hear but has parents who are deaf may be exposed to less spoken language than other children of the same age. Because of this, the child would be at risk for developing a language delay.

Developmental Delay: a term used when a child's development in one or more areas is not progressing at a typical rate, even when keeping in mind the great variety of rates at which children develop. For example, a 14-month-old who is not yet crawling may be considered to have a motor delay. Sometimes doctors will describe a child as having a developmental delay when they have identified a concern in a child's developmental progress, but are waiting to see if the child will eventually "catch up" to her peers in terms of development. If the child does not seem to be progressing, a more specific diagnosis may later be explored. Developmental delays are often seen in the following areas:

- ✦ Cognitive
- ✦ Motor
- ✦ Sensory (including vision and hearing)
- ✦ Communication/Language
- ✦ Social/Emotional
- ✦ Adaptive (self-help)

Early Intervention: a term that describes services provided by specialists to infants and toddlers (birth to 36 months) with special needs, with the goal of supporting their development in an area or areas of need.

Important Information about Special Education Law

The federal government has strong laws in place to protect and support individuals with special needs. The Individuals with Disabilities Act of 2004 ensures special education services to all eligible children, including infants and toddlers. It also governs how states and public agencies provide early intervention and other services and includes a federal grant program that provides funding to assist those organizations providing these services. Individual states decide whether they will provide services only to those with a diagnosed disability or developmental delay, or if they will also provide services to children with at-risk conditions. States also must designate a lead agency to manage referrals and determine eligibility, and are required to provide a toll-free phone number to assist providers and families through the referral process. If you have questions about this process or eligibility requirements in your state, contact your state's designated lead agency. A quick online search or call to a local pediatrician's office should get you the toll-free phone number and agency name.

Observing Infants

Observant caregivers like you play an important role in the early identification of the possibility of special needs. The attention and care you give each infant will enable you to really get to know an individual child's strengths and weaknesses, likes and dislikes. It is likely you also have the unique advantage of having a lot of experience with many different children of the same age. Your knowledge of typical development in infants (keeping in mind the great variety of ages at which typical children achieve developmental milestones), combined with your experience, may put you in a position to notice a child whose development does not seem to be following the typical path. This is often referred to as "atypical development."

Despite your desire to do what is best for the child, and your strong belief that there may be an issue that needs to be explored, sharing your concern with parents is daunting. It is helpful to have already built a strong relationship with families when you do decide to share your concerns. When the child you are concerned about is not well supported at home or has an inconsistent or even volatile home life, the family member—caregiver relationship is often challenging, but in these situations a positive relationship with the family is especially important and deserves extra effort. Relationships with families grow when you communicate regularly and openly, share positive moments as much as possible, and are honest about issues that arise. Doing so helps family members to value your opinion and trust your judgment.

Even if you feel secure in the relationship that you have built with a family, approach them with care. An issue that may seem obvious to you might have gone completely unnoticed by parents. Even if family members suspect something, no one wants to hear from someone else that their child may have a special need. Being faced with this idea is a huge emotional strain, and many families flat out reject the notion right away. Do not be surprised or offended if they are skeptical or want a second opinion. Your concerns can bring up a variety of emotions and self-doubt in family members. They are probably worried about what the future holds for their child as well as for the rest of the family, and they may question their abilities as parents.

Sometimes sharing your concerns will end up only planting the seed that there may be an issue. Most parents will need time to come to terms with the idea and act on it.

Below are some of the more common special needs identified in infants.

Motor Delays	✿ weak or inconsistent reflexes
	✿ slow to develop motor skills
Communication Delays	✿ limited attempts to communicate non-verbally or verbally
	✿ lack of babbling or speech-mimicking vocalizations
Social/Emotional Delays	✿ irritable, difficult to nurture
	✿ difficulty forming attachments
Visual Impairments	✿ lack of interest in objects
	✿ doesn't reach for or search out objects
Hearing Impairments	✿ lack of reaction to sounds
	✿ surprised by "sudden appearance" of others
	✿ babbling may begin then stop

Early intervention is important no matter what issues you believe a child may have. Whatever their disabilities may be, all children have abilities. Early intervention builds upon these abilities and helps their young brains make important connections that will help these children to compensate as they grow.

Meeting Infants' Needs

Once a professional has identified an infant as having special needs, you may feel concerned and possibly overwhelmed. Try to think of this information as simply background information or a context in which to view the infant. Do not define the child by his needs. Take the time to really understand him as an individual. It may take extra time and effort, depending upon the child and the nature of his needs, but learn his strengths and interests as well or better than you would any other child. This knowledge will be helpful when working with his family and caring for him.

A child with identified special needs may come to your program with an Individualized Family Service Plan (IFSP) already in place. This is a plan put together by a team that includes parents and often specialists, doctors and nurses, social workers, and educators. It usually contains the infant's current developmental information, general developmental goals, and specific objectives to meet those goals and evaluate progress. This plan can be very helpful to you. It will help you understand the child's needs and abilities, and it can also be useful when thinking of individual goals for the child in your program. If an infant has recently been diagnosed as having special needs and does not have a plan, you may want to suggest to parents that they talk to their doctor or specialist about creating one.

Remember, you are not expected to be an expert, specialist, or therapist. Your job is to provide all infants with a caring, nurturing environment that encourages them to grow, explore, and develop. Use the resources available to you to create an environment that is as nonrestrictive as possible. Try to ensure that a child with special needs has all the opportunities to participate in activities, develop relationships, and enjoy the experiences that are available to the other children in your program. After all, children with special needs are more similar to their peers than different. They enjoy and benefit from many of the same experiences.

Give yourself a break, and involve the people around you. Use family members as a resource. Chances are that they know quite a bit about their child's condition and needs. With the parents' permission, invite the child's specialists to your program. They may have important advice and insights on ways to make your program even more successful at meeting the needs of the special children in your care.

Adapting Your Environment

Get a new perspective on your environment by looking at it through the eyes of your child or children with special needs. Be aware of texture and audio cues for children who are blind. Can a child who is visually impaired orient herself by noticing that the floor changes from carpet to a hard surface as she moves from the play area to the food area? Can you play soft, soothing music in the quiet space to help her identify that area? Be aware of the acoustics of your space for children who are hearing-impaired. Too much background noise could make it hard for these children to focus on specific sounds. Children who are tactile-defensive are very sensitive to textures and touch sensations. They may become overwhelmed or upset by textures or tactile experiences that many children enjoy or experience without incident, including playing in sand, finger painting, handling textured toys and certain fabrics, and so on. Can you provide tools to help children who are tactile-defensive explore these materials more comfortably?

There is a lot of equipment out there that is especially designed for children with different disabilities. Much of this equipment can also be useful for children who may have less severe developmental issues. Bolsters (cylindrical cushions) and wedges are very helpful for positioning children who have difficulty sitting or lying on their stomachs or sides. These special cushions help to prop children up in a way that encourages them to explore and develop their skills. Consider other items:

- Gloves, sticks, and paintbrushes for children who are tactile-defensive
- Large crayons and markers or even Velcro straps for children with fine motor issues

Being an Effective Caregiver

To be an effective caregiver of a child with special needs, you should learn as much as you can about the child and her condition. Remember to use parents as a resource. Ask them to recommend other resources to help you learn more. Most important, keep the lines of communication wide open. Work as a team with family members and the other professionals in the child's life. The more you learn about the child, the more successfully you will be able to address her needs. Adapt your program, but avoid overprotecting the child. Just like all children, those with special needs need to be challenged and have opportunities to problem-solve without getting too frustrated.

Caring for a child with special needs can be challenging. Recognize your own feelings. Acknowledging and talking about them with the other people you work with can help you to resolve or move past these feelings. Developing a strong relationship and supporting the growth and development of a child with special needs—or any child—is very rewarding. Each milestone, every achievement, brings with it great joy and a sense of accomplishment for the child, her family, and for you.

Activities

To help you create learning experiences that support the development of the infants in your care, the remainder of this book is devoted to developmentally appropriate and engaging activity experiences. As you flip through the various activities, think about the ages and developmental interests of the infants. Do you have a child who loves to explore textures? Perhaps one of the infants is on the verge of crawling, and you'd like to provide an experience that will encourage this. Look for activities that fit the developmental ages and unique interests of individual infants.

The activities are divided according to developmental area, and go in chronological order according to age to help you quickly find activities that will meet the interests and ages of the children. Remember, all children develop at different rates, so it is not uncommon to have an eight-month-old child who is interested in the language activities for a six-to-nine-month-old but the motor activities for a twelve-to-eighteen-month-old. You will also notice that each activity provides a brief explanation of its benefits. All of the activity experiences in this book list multiple areas of development in the Benefits section, because infant development is so interconnected. Do not be surprised if the infant is particularly interested in one area or aspect of the activity over the others. This is common.

In addition to an explanation of the activity and its benefits, each also includes information about what to look for as you watch a child engage in the activity experience. These questions help to focus your attention on key expectations of child engagement and can help you to understand how an individual child is working through the developmental milestones. Finally, each activity includes a Tips section, which you will find useful to help you modify the activity for different ages, abilities, or interests.

Resources

Dombro, A. L., Colker, L. J., and Trister Dodge, D. 1999. *The creative curriculum for infants and toddlers*. Bethesda, MD: Teaching Strategies, Inc.

Gonzalez-Mena, J., and Widmeyer Eyer, D. 2008. *Infants, toddlers, and caregivers*. Columbus, OH: McGraw-Hill.

Greenman, J., and Stonehouse, A. 2002. *Prime times: A handbook for excellence in infant and toddler care*. St. Paul, MN: Redleaf Press.

National Association for the Education of Young Children. 2007. *NAEYC early childhood program standards and accreditation criteria: The mark of quality*. Washington, DC: National Association for the Education of Young Children.

National Center for Infants, Toddlers, and Families. www.zerotothree.org

National Institute for Child and Human Development. Positional plagiocephaly. Retrieved on July 12, 2011, from http://www.nichd.nih.gov/health/topics/positional_plagiocephaly.cfm

U.S. Department of Education. Building the Legacy: IDEA 2004. http://idea.ed.gov

Willis, C. 2009. *Teaching infants, toddlers, and twos with special needs*. Silver Spring, MD: Gryphon House, Inc.

Tell Me Everything

What to do

1. While you are having an experience with baby (diapering, cuddling, walking around), keep a running monologue going. Tell baby what you are doing. Describe what you see, smell, or feel. Describe what he is doing.
2. Make sure that your facial expressions and tone of voice match your words. If you are happy, excited, worried, or upset, send the signal loud and clear with your voice, words, and face.

What to look for

* Does baby maintain eye contact?
* Does he react differently to your different tones or facial expressions?

Tips

* Use this activity to help soothe baby. Let him know when you are approaching him, what you are going to do (change his diaper, feed him), and tell him what you are doing as you make your way to him.
* Mix your running monologue with some baby babble time!

Social and Emotional ☺☹

6 weeks+

Anywhere

Prep Time ⏱ **None**

Benefits
* Promotes bonding
* Develops language and listening skills

Materials
✓ None

Soothing Touch

What to do

1. Gently massage baby's hands and arms.
2. Make this a special, soothing time by focusing on the child as you gently rub each finger, hand, and arm.

What to look for

❀ How does baby react to the rubbing? Does she focus on your face as you rub her? Does she relax?

❀ If you've chosen a consistent time or place where you do the massage, does she begin to show signs of anticipation?

Tips

❀ Use this activity to help soothe a fussy baby. Even older children find hand massage calming.

❀ Enhance the sensory experience by rubbing baby with scented lotion or oil. Singing or humming a lullaby can also add to the experience.

Note: *Some babies have very sensitive skin and may have unknown allergies. If bumps, welts, or redness appear after using lotion on baby, clean her skin immediately and document the reaction for families.*

Social and Emotional ☺☹

6 weeks+

Anywhere

Prep Time ⏱ **None**

Benefits
❀ Promotes bonding
❀ Encourages sensory stimulation
❀ Calms and soothes children

Materials
☑ None

Soothing Baby Lotion

Peekaboo

What to do

1. Sit across from baby, and make eye contact.
2. Cover your eyes with your hands, then uncover them, say, "Peekaboo!" and smile.
3. Repeat for as long as the child is interested.

What to look for

✿ Does the child anticipate your actions?
✿ How does baby react? Does he smile or laugh? Open his eyes wide? Look surprised or frightened? Remember, if a child reacts negatively to an activity, stop doing the activity with the child. You can try again later.

Tips

✿ Instead of using your hands, cover your face with other materials, for example, a blanket or scarf, or hide behind furniture, and so on.
✿ Cover and uncover baby's eyes and watch the reaction.
✿ Encourage older babies to lead the peekaboo game.
✿ Read books with a peekaboo theme, such as *Farm Peekaboo!* by Charlie Gardner.

Social and Emotional ☺☹

3+ months

Anywhere

Prep Time ⏱ **None**

Benefits
✿ Promotes social interaction
✿ Baby learns to anticipate actions based on experience

Materials
☑ None

Silly Faces

What to do

1. While you are sitting with or holding baby, look into her eyes and make a silly face.
2. Hold your silly expression for a moment to give baby a chance to take it in and react.
3. Continue with other silly faces for as long as baby is interested.

What to look for

✿ How does baby react? Does she smile or laugh?
✿ Does baby reach for your face?

Tips

✿ If baby doesn't have much of a reaction, it may be that she can't see your face clearly. Move your face a little closer to hers. If she reacts strongly in a negative way (looking away, fussing), you may be too close. Move back a bit.
✿ When baby smiles or otherwise has a positive reaction to the face you have made, hold your face still and within her reach to allow her to explore it with her hands or arms.

Social and Emotional ☺☹

3+ months

Anywhere

Prep Time ⊘ **None**

Benefits
✿ Promotes social interaction

Materials
☑ None

Family Wall

What to do

1. Find a spot on the wall at child height where you can display family photos. Preferably, the wall should be located in a quiet activity area.
2. Use the contact paper to cover the photos. Leave at least an inch of contact paper all around each photo to stick the photo to the wall.
3. Show babies the photos.

What to look for

✿ Do the children enjoy looking at the faces in the photos?
✿ Do the children recognize their families? Remember, even photos are abstract representations of people, so while babies may enjoy looking at the faces, they may not recognize who the faces represent.

Tips

✿ Make sure the photos are large enough that individuals can be easily identified.
✿ Leave enough space between photos for several children to look at once.
✿ Make a family nook, and include something from the home of each child.

Social and Emotional ☺☹

6+ months

Indoors

Prep Time ⏱ **15 minutes**

Benefits
✿ Strengthens the mutual family-caregiver relationship
✿ Promotes positive self-esteem

Materials
☑ Photo of each child's family
☑ Clear contact paper

Pounce!

What to do

1. Sit across from baby, and make eye contact.
2. With an excited expression on your face, slowly walk your hands across the floor toward her. Say, "Walking… walking… walking…"
3. When you are about to reach baby's feet, quickly grab her toes, and say, "Pounce!"
4. Repeat for as long as she is interested.

What to look for

✿ How does baby react to your first pounce? Does she startle? smile?
✿ Does she begin to anticipate the pounce when you begin walking your fingers?

Tips

✿ Try this activity by walking a small stuffed animal instead of your fingers.
✿ Walk your fingers up baby's arm or legs, and pounce onto other parts of her body (head, shoulder, knee, belly).
✿ Encourage older infants to play the game pouncing at you.

Social and Emotional ☺☹

6+ months

Anywhere

Prep Time ⏲ **None**

Benefits

✿ Promotes social interaction
✿ Baby learns to anticipate actions based on experience

Materials

☑ None

Hello and Goodbye

What to do

1. When a child or another person enters the room, say, "Hello, _____!" and wave.
2. When someone leaves, say, "Goodbye, _____!" and wave.
3. Encourage baby to wave with you.

What to look for

* Does baby wave, with encouragement?
* Does he begin to wave and greet people on his own?
* How do children react to being greeted?

Tips

* Turn this into a game by repeatedly entering and leaving the room, waving and saying hello and goodbye.
* Make a stuffed animal or doll appear and disappear. Wave and say hello and goodbye to the doll.

Social and Emotional ☺☹

6+ months

Anywhere

Prep Time ⊕ **None**

Benefits
* Promotes social ritual
* Develops positive self-esteem in children being greeted

Materials
☑ None

Group Photo Album

What to do

1. Place photos in the photo book.
2. If you are making your own book, follow these steps:

   ✿ Place photos on each side of your construction paper (the fewer photos to a page, the better), and cover each page completely with contact paper.

   ✿ Punch two to three holes along one side of each completed page.

   ✿ Fasten the pages together with the yarn or other binding material.

3. Sit with a child, and encourage her to flip through the pages of the class book.

What to look for

✿ Does the child enjoy looking at the faces of others?
✿ Does the child recognize herself or others?
✿ Does she point to the actual person after seeing the photograph?

Tips

✿ Use close-up images that do not have a busy background to help children focus on faces.
✿ Younger children will enjoy looking at one photo to a page, while older children will enjoy flipping through the album and pointing to children you name.

Social and Emotional ☺☹

9+ months

Indoors

Prep Time ⊕ **25 minutes**

Benefits

✿ **Strengthens group relationship**
✿ **Promotes positive self-esteem**

Materials

☑ **Close-up photo of each person in the group, including staff, frequent visitors, familiar family members, and group pets**
☑ **Commercially available photo book or**

   ✿ Clear contact paper
   ✿ Construction paper
   ✿ Hole punch
   ✿ Yarn or book-binding material

Hands on Hands

What to do

1. When baby's hand is flat on a surface, place your hand gently over hers.
2. If she moves her hand away, place your hand on the surface, and invite her to put her hand on yours. If she does not remove her hand from under yours, place your other hand on top of the hand pile.
3. Invite her to add to the hand pile with her hand.
4. When all hands are in the pile, say, "Hooray!" and give her hands a gentle squeeze before pulling your hands away.

What to look for

* Does baby react positively to this game of touch?
* After being exposed to the game, does she participate independently?
* Does she initiate the game or indicate that she would like to continue?

Tips

* Some children prefer firm touch while others prefer light touch. Explore both with baby.
* You can make this game more challenging for older infants by making sure you and baby alternate hands. Eventually you can try pulling out your hand and placing it on top, and then encourage baby to do the same.

Social and Emotional ☺☹

9+ months

Anywhere

Prep Time ⊙ **None**

Benefits
* Promotes positive social interaction
* Develops fine motor skills

Materials
☑ None

Floor Catch

What to do

1. Sit across from baby with your legs spread out to keep the ball from rolling too far away.
2. Gently roll the ball to the child.
3. Encourage him to push it back toward you.
4. Continue for as long as he remains interested.

What to look for

✿ Does the child anticipate the ball's approach?
✿ After being shown how to push the ball, does he push it on his own?

Tips

✿ Vary the speed at which you push the ball. Does baby react?
✿ With younger babies, find another adult or older child to play with, and nestle the young infant in your lap. He will enjoy watching the ball roll back and forth.

Social and Emotional ☺☹

12+ months

Indoors

Prep Time ⏲ **None**

Benefits
✿ Promotes social interaction
✿ Develops gross motor skills

Materials
☑ Ball or rolling rattle

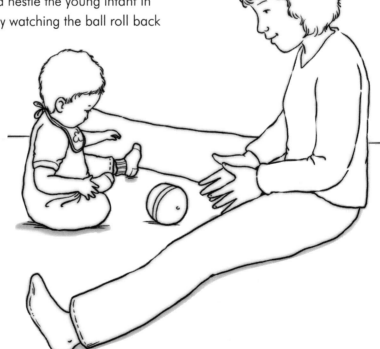

Here I Am!

What to do

1. Cover each photo with contact paper on both sides.
2. Fasten the hooked side of a strip of Velcro to the back of each photo.
3. Place the bin of photos near the felt board.
4. Invite children to find their photos in the bin and stick them to the felt board.

What to look for

* Does the child recognize herself in the photo? Does she recognize others?
* Is the child able to add and remove her photo independently?

Tips

* Make this a morning sign-in ritual. As children post their pictures, talk with them about other children who are here and those who are missing.
* Name different children, and encourage each child to look for the appropriate pictures.

Social and Emotional ☺☹

12+ months

Indoors

Prep Time ⏱ **25 minutes**

Benefits
* Encourages positive self-esteem
* Promotes awareness of others
* Promotes fine motor skills

Materials
☑ Photo of each child
☑ Clear contact paper
☑ Adhesive Velcro strips
☑ Felt board
☑ Bin for storing photos

Feel Better

What to do

1. When a child in the group is injured or upset, as you comfort the child, involve other children.
2. Encourage other children to help. Ask them to bring the upset child a favorite toy or blanket, or show them how to rub the child's back and give words of comfort.
3. Acknowledge and thank the children for their help.

What to look for

* How do the other children react to the upset child?
* Do the children begin to comfort friends independently?
* How does the upset child respond to the help of his peers?

Tips

* Encourage pretend play by acting distressed yourself or having a stuffed animal cry. Help children think of ways to comfort the stuffed animal.
* Label specific feelings. Move beyond sad and mad. Verbalize feelings of frustration, disappointment, and so on.

Social and Emotional ☺☹

12+ months

Anywhere

Prep Time ⏱ **None**

Benefits
* Develops empathy
* Promotes social skills
* Fosters self-esteem

Materials
☑ None

Baby Babble

What to do

1. Make eye contact and speak to baby. Repeat baby's sounds, or start simple conversations: "Don't you look happy today?" "Did you have a good nap?" or "Is that your snuggle bear (or other object) in your hand?" "You love that bear, don't you?" "It is very soft!"
2. Pause after each question or phrase.
3. If baby makes a sound, repeat what she says, then pause and give her another turn to speak.
4. Continue for as long as you both remain interested.

What to look for

✿ Does baby maintain eye contact while you speak to her?
✿ Does she vocalize in response to your sounds?
✿ After she speaks, does she seem to wait for you to speak again?

Tips

✿ Try this activity during diapering, when both you and baby can really focus on one another.
✿ Older infants love to experiment with sounds. Jump in and explore silly sounds and sound patterns with them!
✿ For newborns this activity is a bonding experience, but do not expect them to make many sounds. By two or three months most infants will begin to have "conversations" with you.

Language 🗣

6 weeks+

Anywhere

Prep Time ⏱ **None**

Benefits
✿ Encourages understanding of conversational rhythms
✿ Promotes bonding

Materials
☑ None

Book Nook

What to do

1. Find a cozy place to sit with baby. It may be in a rocking chair, nestled into pillows, or under a tree outside.
2. Snuggle with baby and, if baby is interested, show him the board book. Encourage him to explore it. Show him how the pages open, and point out the pictures.
3. Read the book while cuddling, but be aware of the child's interest. If he is only interested in turning pages, that's okay!

What to look for

- ✿ Does baby enjoy the quiet together time?
- ✿ Does he enjoy exploring the book?
- ✿ Does he notice familiar objects or textures in the pictures?

Tips

- ✿ It is especially important that infants associate books with positive feelings. Cuddling and together time are just as important, if not more important, than actually reading the pages.
- ✿ Choose books that feature pictures of familiar objects that babies can point out. Babies especially love pictures of other babies. Interactive books and repetitive text also work well.
- ✿ Even newborns will benefit from the snuggling and language that they hear while you read.

Language 🗣

6 weeks+

Anywhere

Prep Time 🕐 **5 min**

Benefits
- ✿ **Promotes love of reading**
- ✿ **Encourages bonding**
- ✿ **Develops language**

Materials
- ☑ **Board book**

Eyes and Nose

What to do

1. Angle mirror so that baby can see her reflection.
2. Touch baby's nose while you are both looking at your reflections. Say, "Nose."
3. Touch baby's mouth and say, "Mouth."
4. Continue with the other parts of the face.

What to look for

* Does baby follow your finger in the mirror (or look back and forth between your finger and the mirror image) until it touches her?
* Does she begin to anticipate your touch?
* Watch to see if baby looks away. This may mean that she is disinterested.
* When you pause, does she urge you to continue with her own vocalizations or other signals?

Tips

* Move baby's hands to touch the parts of her face as you name them.
* Encourage older infants to touch the parts of their faces or yours as you say the names for them.
* Add more language to the game by asking baby, "Where is your…" or "What's that? It is your…"

Language

3+ months

Anywhere

Prep Time ⏲ **None**

Benefits
* ❀ Promotes language
* ❀ Develops vision
* ❀ Encourages self-awareness

Materials
* ☑ Unbreakable mirror

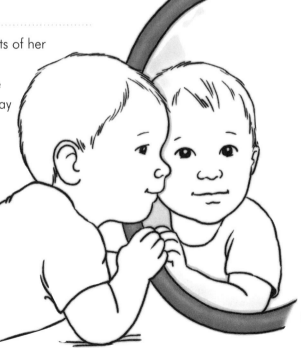

Coo to You, Too!

What to do

1. At the changing table, while holding baby, or any other time that you have baby's full attention, look baby in the eye and make any cooing or nonsense sound.
2. Listen for baby to respond with a sound, and repeat baby's sound, then listen again.
3. Continue repeating baby's sounds for as long as he is interested.

What to look for

✿ Does baby maintain eye contact with you?
✿ Does he mimic your sounds?
✿ Does baby engage in conversational patterns (make a sound, pause and wait for you, respond with a sound)?

Tips

✿ Try this activity imitating baby's gestures rather than vocalizations. Pause and see if baby reacts with another gesture.
✿ If baby looks away or becomes agitated, stop the activity as this is a sign that he is becoming overstimulated.

Language ✿

3+ months

Anywhere

Prep Time ⏱ **None**

Benefits
✿ Encourages vocalizations
✿ Promotes social interaction

Materials
☑ None

Sounds of Home

What to do

1. Ask each family to record themselves singing or speaking to their child.
2. Set up the recordings to play in a quiet area, and give each child the opportunity to listen to his family member's voice.

   Note: *Make sure the recording device is safely out of baby's reach.*

What to look for

✿ Does baby respond to the sound of a familiar voice?

Tips

✿ Introduce this activity when baby is happy and eager to try something new. If the child responds well to the voices, try this activity to help soothe the child during moments of distress, including the morning transition into your program.

✿ Include family photos in the quiet area for children to look at with you as you sit together and listen to the recorded voices.

6+ months

Anywhere

Prep Time ⏱ 10 minutes

Benefits
✿ Develops language
✿ Encourages home-center cooperation
✿ Promotes emotional well-being

Materials
☑ Recording device

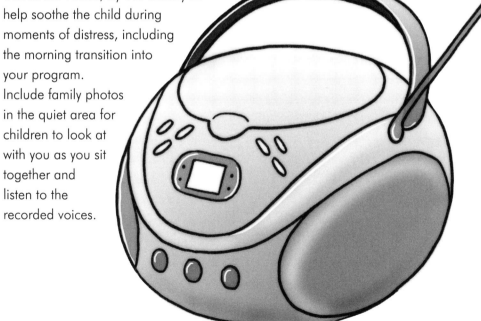

Rhythmic Rhymes

Language 🗣

6+ months

Anywhere

Prep Time 🕐 None

Benefits
✿ **Promotes language development**
✿ **Encourages gross motor movement**

Materials
☑ **None**

What to do

1. Recite any rhyme with a strong rhythm to baby. Nursery rhymes work well. For example:

   Jack and Jill
   Went up the hill
   To fetch a pail of water.
   Jack fell down
   And broke his crown,
   And Jill came tumbling after.

2. Maintain eye contact with baby as you recite the rhyme, and emphasize the rhythm with your voice or actions, such as bouncing up and down, moving baby's arms to the rhythm, and so on.

What to look for

✿ Does baby maintain eye contact while you are speaking?
✿ Does she react to your words and your attention with a smile, positive gesture, or "words" of her own?
✿ Does baby move to the rhythm of your words?

Tips

✿ Emphasize the rhythm even more strongly by clapping as you recite the rhyme. Encourage baby to clap, too!
✿ If baby's home language is different from your own, ask families to share a simple rhyme in their native language with you. Learn it and recite it to baby.

Which Is Winnie?

What to do

1. Sit baby down so that she is surrounded by a few (no more than three to avoid overwhelming the child) familiar toys or people.
2. Ask her, "Which is Winnie?" (or the name of another person or object).
3. After a moment, point to one object and ask, "Is this Winnie?" Pause and move on to the next object. "Is this Winnie?" Pause again and move on to the object named Winnie.
4. Say, "Oh, here is Winnie!" and touch or pick up Winnie the teddy bear.
5. Continue with the other objects for as long as the child is interested.

What to look for

✿ Does baby look toward or point at the object you named?
✿ Does she react when you reach for the wrong object?
✿ Does she get excited as you reach for the correct object?

Tips

✿ With younger children, begin with just one or two objects.
✿ Encourage mobile infants to crawl to the item you have named.

Language ✿

6+ months

Anywhere

Prep Time ⏱ **5 minutes**

Benefits
✿ Develops vocabulary

Materials
☑ A few very familiar toys or people

Nonsense Song

What to do

1. Think of any tune you know, and substitute repetitive nonsense sounds for the lyrics. For example, "Twinkle, Twinkle, Little Star" would become "Ba-ba, ba-ba, ba-ba ba."
2. Look baby in the eye, and sing this nonsense song.

What to look for

✿ Does baby respond or react with any sounds of his own?
✿ Does he move to the rhythm of the tune?

Tips

✿ Experiment with different nonsense sounds and different tunes to see if baby responds more to a particular type of sound or rhythm. Babies need to practice and explore a variety of sounds before they are ready to put the sounds together to say words.

Language ✿

6+ months

Anywhere

Prep Time ⊙ **None**

Benefits
✿ Encourages vocalizations

Materials
☑ None

Baby Signs

What to do

1. Use simple gestures to represent common words like juice, more, hungry, wet, and so on. (For pictures of suggested signs, see the next page.)
2. Introduce one sign at a time by using the gesture every time you say the word.
3. When baby begins to use the gesture, give him positive reinforcement by immediately letting him know that you understand what he is communicating.
4. Begin by using one or two signs regularly, then slowly add more to baby's sign vocabulary.

What to look for

* Is baby able to make the gestures for the signs?
* Does he use the signs to communicate?
* Does he begin to create his own signs? Be on the lookout for this, and incorporate his signs into your vocabulary!

Tips

* Encourage other staff and family members to use the signs with the child.
* Create name signs for the children in your group.
* Look for children's books that feature signing, to increase your sign vocabulary.
* Signing and gestures enable babies to communicate successfully long before their vocal cords and muscle control allow them to talk. Rather than delaying speech, signing seems to encourage communication, which can lead to early speech and improved vocabulary.

Language

9+ months

Anywhere

Prep Time ⏲ **None**

Benefits
* Develops vocabulary
* Encourages communication
* Promotes fine motor skills

Materials
☑ None

Baby Signs

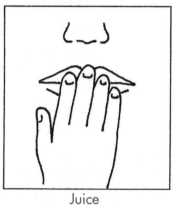
Eat
Hand places food in mouth.

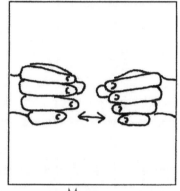
Juice
Fingers tap mouth.

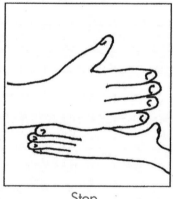
More
Fingers and thumbs pinched together. Touch fingertips together.

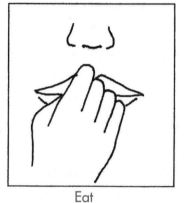
All Done
Hands shake back and forth.

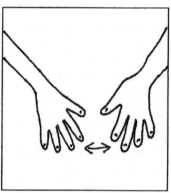
Stop
Edge of one hand comes down on palm.

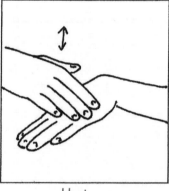
Hurt
Fingers of one hand tap the back of the other.

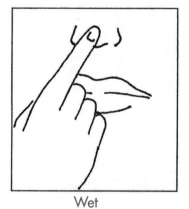
Wet
Index finger touches nose.

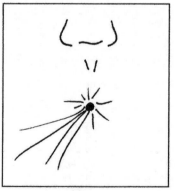
Hot
Blow gently.

Out
Elbow bent, finger points away from body.

Tube Talkers

What to do

1. Hold the paper tube to your mouth, and talk through it. Change your voice. Speak in various pitches. Whisper.
2. Give the tube to an infant, and encourage the child to make sounds into the tube.

What to look for

- ✿ How does baby react when she hears you or her own voice through the tube?
- ✿ How else does the child explore the tube?

Tips

- ✿ Invite older infants to experiment with shorter and longer tubes.
- ✿ Put your hand over the end of the tube as you talk into it, then remove your hand. Does baby respond to the change in sound? Does she try to cover the tube with her own hand?

Language 🗣

9+ months

Anywhere

Prep Time ⏱ **5 minutes**

Benefits
- ✿ Promotes exploration of language

Materials
- ☑ Paper towel or gift wrap tube

Pack It Up

What to do

1. Set out an open suitcase, and begin packing the familiar objects.
2. When children approach to see what you are doing, explain that you would like some help packing some things into the suitcase.
3. Ask a child to bring you a familiar, nearby item. Use directional words, for example, "Niko, please bring me the doll lying next to the cradle."
4. Thank the child for the item, and put the item in the suitcase.
5. Continue asking for specific items for as long as children remain interested.

What to look for

- Is the child able to identify the item you named?
- Does the child respond to your directions?
- Does he help you place the items in the suitcase?

Tips

- To build vocabulary, pack up related items, for example, clothes, animals, and so on.
- Use a puppet as the packer. Children often respond well to puppets. The puppet can help the child find an item if he is having trouble.
- Unpack the bag, and name each item as you remove it.
- Try this activity with boxes or baskets at cleanup time.

Language 🗨

12+ months

Anywhere

Prep Time ⏱ **10 minutes**

Benefits
- ✿ **Develops language and vocabulary**
- ✿ **Encourages cooperation**

Materials
- ☑ **Bag, box, or suitcase**
- ☑ **Items to pack**

Animal Sounds

What to do

1. As you look at pictures of animals with an infant, name the animal and make the sound the animal makes.

What to look for

- Does the child imitate the animal sound? Can she name the animal?
- Does the child begin to associate the animals' pictures with their sounds?

Tips

- Add a movement component. Show the child how the animal moves, and encourage her to imitate you.
- Use stuffed animals or plastic animals rather than pictures.
- Take a trip to a zoo to see the real animals. Be sure to make the visit short and sweet.

Language 🗣

12+ months

Anywhere

Prep Time ⏲ **5 minutes**

Benefits
- ✿ Develops language
- ✿ Encourages the imitation of sound for speech

Materials
- ☑ Pictures of animals

Picture Cards

What to do

1. Use the contact paper to laminate individual pictures of familiar items onto the index cards.
2. Place the pictures in a basket, and make them available to the children.
3. Invite children to empty the basket and look at the pictures.
4. Talk about or name the items as the children look at them.
5. Encourage the children to point to items that you name.

What to look for

✿ Does the child name the item pictured?
✿ How else does he use the picture cards?

Tips

✿ Try to find images of items with no background, or cut the background away to reduce the visual clutter for children.
✿ Make a matching game with older children by using pictures of items in the room. They can match the pictures to real objects.
✿ Have different groups of cards, for example, animal cards, toy cards, people cards, and so on.

Language 🗣

12+ months

Anywhere

Prep Time 🕐 **10 minutes**

Benefits
✿ **Builds vocabulary**

Materials
☑ **Pictures of familiar items cut out of magazines**
☑ **Index cards**
☑ **Clear contact paper**
☑ **Basket to store pictures**

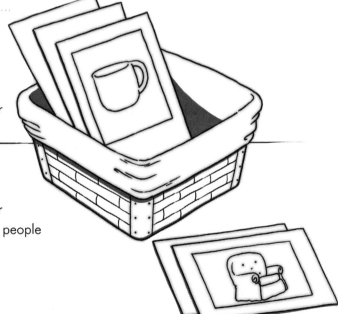

Tiny Touch

What to do

1. While holding baby in your arms or lap, present the object to her.
2. If she does not reach out for it, gently guide her hand to it, or softly rub it against her hand.
3. Invite her to explore the surface with her fingers.

What to look for

* Does she move her fingers to explore the object?
* Does she grasp at it?

Tips

* Place object in front of baby for her to explore at tummy time.
* Promote language skills and bonding by talking to baby while she is touching the object. Describe what she is doing or ask her questions, for example, "Does that feel soft?"
* Make sure that the objects you present to baby are clean. Sanitize items with a solution of ¾ cup household bleach to one gallon of water. Rinse thoroughly before presenting to baby. Washing items in very hot water (at least 130 degrees) will also sanitize objects.

Motor 🖐

6 weeks+

Anywhere

Prep Time ⏱ **5 minutes**

Benefits
* **Develops fine motor skills**
* **Promotes sensory development (tactile)**

Materials
☑ **Textured object (for example, a rough-textured item like a washcloth, a smooth item such as a metal spoon, or a bristled item such as a new toothbrush)**

Wriggling Ribbons

What to do

1. Knot the middle of each ribbon to the ring so that you have two ribbon "tails" of approximately equal lengths.
2. Place baby on the floor on his back.
3. Hold the ring and dangle the ribbons over baby. Begin holding the ribbons about one foot above baby. Then raise or lower the ribbons to get a reaction from baby and encourage him to reach for the ribbons.
4. Wriggle the ribbons, and slide them across his body and arms.

What to look for

✿ Does baby follow the ribbons with his eyes?
✿ Does he grasp at the ribbons?
✿ How does he react when you pull the ribbons away then bring them close again?

Tips

✿ Dangle the ribbons in front of baby at tummy time (see page 9 for more information about tummy time). Does he reach for them?
✿ With very young infants, use ribbons of strongly contrasting colors (black and white, bright purple and yellow, and so on).
✿ Try tying strips of other textured material to the ring.

Motor 🖐

3+ months

Anywhere

Prep Time 🕐 **5 minutes**

Benefits
✿ **Develops fine motor skills and coordination**
✿ **Promotes sensory development (visual, tactile)**

Materials
☑ **Medium-sized ring (stiff bracelet, plastic lid with center removed, and so on)**
☑ **Several ribbons (about one-foot lengths)**

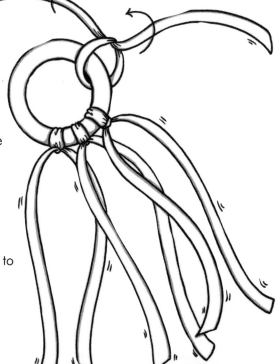

Pull It Close

What to do

1. Place baby on her tummy and put the pull toy near baby but out of reach.
2. Draw baby's attention to the toy by shaking or rolling it, then use the string to pull the toy close.
3. Put the toy back in its original spot, then hand the string to baby.
4. Encourage her to pull the toy close.
5. If baby is having trouble pulling the string and showing signs of becoming frustrated (frantic movements or agitated noises), help her to be successful by guiding her hand in pulling the toy, or by pushing the toy toward her.
6. Continue for as long as she remains interested.

What to look for

* How does baby react when the toy comes close? Does she smile or get excited?
* Is she able to manipulate the string?
* Does the child grasp the concept of pulling the string to bring the toy closer?

Tips

* This is a great activity for tummy time (see page 9 for more information about tummy time).
* You may need to pull the toy close several times before baby attempts it herself.
* A shorter string will give baby more immediate gratification.
* Encourage mobile infants to crawl while holding the string. Watch them as they discover the toy is following them!

Motor 🖑

3+ months

Anywhere

Prep Time ⊘ **5 minutes**

Benefits
* Develops fine and gross motor skills
* Promotes understanding of cause and effect

Materials
☑ Pull toy or short string tied to any wheeled toy

Grab and Squish

What to do

1. Sit with baby during his tummy time (see page 9 for more information about tummy time).
2. Hold a soft block where baby can see it, and squeeze or shake it to make a noise.
3. Once the block has caught baby's attention, set the block far enough from baby that he needs to reach to grab it.
4. If baby loses interest once the block is on the ground, shake it or squeeze it again, keeping it close to the ground.
5. Continue encouraging baby until he attempts to reach the block. If he continues to have trouble after a few attempts, help him out.
6. Once he grabs the block, celebrate his success!

What to look for

✿ Does baby react to the noise the block makes?
✿ Does he lift his upper body and attempt to reach for the block?
✿ Does the child try to create a sound by squeezing or shaking the block?

Tips

✿ Use several different blocks that make different noises or are different shapes, colors, sizes, or textures. Does the child show a preference?
✿ Hold the block, and as you squeeze or shake it, move it closer to baby. Does he reach for it as it gets closer?
✿ Encourage baby to roll over by holding the block just out of reach when baby is on his back, then slowly move the block across his body. As he twists to reach for it, he will build the muscles he needs to roll over.

Motor 🖐

3+ months

Anywhere

Prep Time ⏱ 5 minutes

Benefits
✿ **Develops gross motor skills**
✿ **Encourages sensory development**
✿ **Promotes understanding of cause and effect**

Materials
☑ **Soft sound-making objects**

Tumbling Towers

What to do

1. Make a wide block tower near baby but out of her reach.
2. Give baby a ball or other object to throw.
3. Help baby to throw the ball toward the tower. If she misses, get the ball for her, and invite her to keep trying. Help her get closer to the tower if necessary.
4. Celebrate with her when she successfully hits the tower and knocks the blocks down.

What to look for

* Is baby able to throw the object?
* How does baby react when the blocks tumble? Is she surprised, excited, or frightened?
* Does she let you know that she'd like to do it again?

Tips

* Younger infants will need light blocks to be successful. Older infants will enjoy the sound of hard blocks as they tumble.
* Make a large, soft block by stuffing a paper bag with newspaper and topping it with another paper bag. Milk cartons with the tops cut off, one stuffed upside-down inside the other, also work well.
* Create a throwing space with bins, tipped buckets, or hanging scarves as targets. Be consistent about when and where you allow babies to throw.
* Invite older infants to build their own piles of blocks to knock down.

Motor ✋

6+ months

Anywhere

Prep Time ⏱ 5 minutes

Benefits
* Develops gross motor skills
* Develops eye-hand coordination
* Promotes understanding of cause and effect

Materials
* Blocks (the lighter the better)
* Ball or other object to throw

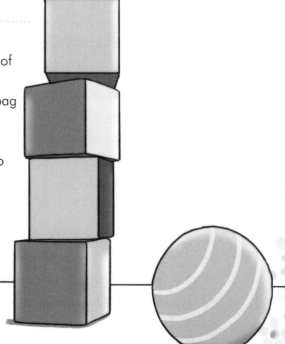

ACTIVITIES

Clap, Hooray!

What to do

1. Whenever baby accomplishes something (reaches a toy he's been trying to reach) or does something and then looks you, respond by saying, "You reached the ball!"
2. Encourage baby to clap and celebrate with you.

What to look for

✿ Does baby react positively to your clapping and positive enthusiasm?
✿ Does he attempt to clap as well?
✿ Does he begin to initiate clapping after an accomplishment?

Tips

✿ Some babies may need you to place your hands over theirs to help them get the feel of clapping. This hand-over-hand support should only be temporary. Baby needs opportunities to practice independently as well.
✿ As baby begins to clap on his own, give him plenty of opportunities to practice. Clap to music, clap to songs you sing, and clap to show your joy at being with baby. Encourage him to clap with you.

Motor 🖐

6+ months

Anywhere

Prep Time ⏱ **None**

Benefits
✿ Develops fine motor skills
✿ Promotes self-esteem

Materials
☑ None

Shake, Rattle, and Drop!

What to do

1. Fill the bin with several rattles, and set the bin near baby.
2. Pull out one of the rattles and shake it. Then drop it back in the bin.
3. Invite baby to reach in and explore the different rattles.

What to look for

✿ How does baby grab the rattles? Does he use one hand or two? Does he shake the rattles with his whole arm, or is he turning his wrist?

✿ Does he dump and fill the rattle bin?

Tips

✿ The bin itself is a wonderful toy. Invite children to fill the bin and dump its contents, push it around, and sit on or in it.

✿ For older infants learning to hold a cup, fill the bin with various nonbreakable cups and other items with handles.

Motor 🖐

6+ months

Anywhere

Prep Time ⏲ **5 minutes**

Benefits
✿ Develops fine motor skills
✿ Promotes sensory awareness (auditory, tactile)

Materials
☑ Plastic bin or shallow tub
☑ Various rattles

Where Did It Go?

What to do

1. Sit baby facing the hole in the box, and focus the child's attention on one of the objects.
2. While baby is watching, drop the object through the hole in the box.
3. Ask, "Where did it go?"
4. Encourage the child to look for the object.

What to look for

✿ Does baby look for the shape in the box?
✿ Does she figure out a way to retrieve the shape?
✿ Does she try putting the shape back into the hole?

Tips

✿ Give children a variety of shapes or objects to fill and then empty in a shape sorter.
✿ If baby does not seem to realize that the object is in the sorter, encourage her to look through the holes to see the missing item. Invite her to reach for it.

Motor 🖐

9+ months

Anywhere

Prep Time ⏱ 5 minutes

Benefits
✿ Develops gross motor skills
✿ Encourages understanding of object permanence
✿ Develops problem-solving skills

Materials
☑ Any box with holes large enough for baby's arm
☑ 2 to 3 objects that fit in the holes

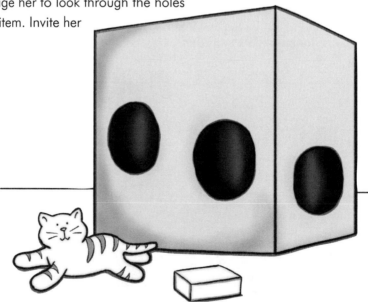

Obstacle Course

What to do

1. Arrange the items around the room so that they are easily accessible to babies.
2. Encourage children to explore crawling over, under, and through the obstacles.

What to look for

- Does baby figure out how to get over, under, and through the obstacles?
- Does baby show a preference for a particular obstacle or movement?
- Does baby explore new ways to use or experience the obstacles?

Tips

- If children are not sure what to make of the obstacle course, crawl through it with them!
- Encourage problem solving. Resist the urge to jump in and rescue children the moment they seem unable to get through an obstacle.
- Entice children by placing favorite toys throughout the obstacle course.
- Do not expect infants to go through an obstacle course following a specific path. Think of the experience as free exploration of the obstacles.

Motor ✋

9+ months

Anywhere

Prep Time ⏱ **10 minutes**

Benefits
- Develops gross motor skills
- Develops eye-hand coordination
- Encourages problem solving

Materials
- ☑ Low platforms, sturdy blocks, thick mats, or other items to crawl over
- ☑ Tunnels, large boxes with tops and bottoms cut out, or other items to crawl through
- ☑ Chairs without low rungs, tables, or other items to crawl under

Box Car

What to do

1. Turn the box upside-down, and set it out in an open space on a smooth floor for baby.
2. Encourage baby to pull up on the box.
   Note: *Sit near baby to help him in case the box tips over or he falls.*
3. Once baby is comfortable and confident while standing, slowly pull the box toward you just a little so that baby has to take a step to continue to hold onto the box.
4. If baby is comfortable with this movement, slowly pull the box farther, encouraging more steps from baby.

What to look for

- ✿ Is baby able to keep his balance as you move the box?
- ✿ Does he begin to push the box on his own?

Tips

- ✿ Do this activity only if baby is able to pull up to standing on his own. Place a favorite toy on top of the box to encourage children to pull themselves up.
- ✿ Set the box on different surfaces. Is he able to push enough to get the box moving on carpet? Can he keep pace with the box when it is on a smooth surface?

Motor ✋

9+ months

Open area

Prep Time ⏱ **5 minutes**

Benefits
- ✿ **Develops gross motor skills**
- ✿ **Promotes understanding of cause and effect**

Materials
- ☑ **Medium-sized cardboard box (should be just about waist-high, or slightly higher, for the infant when standing and wide enough to resist tipping)**

Shake It Up!

What to do

1. Serve baby a small helping of macaroni.
   Note: *Check for food allergies before this or any food-related activity.*
2. Show her how to shake out the cheese, and then give her the cheese shaker.
3. Encourage her to put cheese on her macaroni.
4. Remove the shaker and eat!

What to look for

- Does baby successfully get cheese from the shaker?
- Does she show new interest in her food after helping to prepare it?
- Is she able to manipulate the spoon to eat?

Tips

- If baby does not want to stop shaking out cheese, fill the shaker with only a small amount of cheese.
- Try this activity using applesauce and cinnamon sugar. Make sure the shaker has very small holes!
- Encourage other self-feeding activities, such as dipping bananas into yogurt.

Motor ✋

12+ months

Meal Time

Prep Time ⏲ **5 minutes**

Benefits
- Develops gross motor skills
- Develops self-help skills
- Promotes understanding of cause and effect

Materials
- ☑ Grated cheese in a shaker
- ☑ Bowl of cooked macaroni
- ☑ Spoon

Stack 'Em Up!

What to do

1. Set blocks out for baby to explore.
2. When baby picks up and sets down a block, show her how to stack blocks by placing another block on top of the first block.
3. Encourage her to put another block on top of the second block.
4. Continue for as long as baby is interested.

What to look for

- ✿ Is baby able to successfully manipulate one block on top of another?
- ✿ Does she show pleasure in her accomplishment?
- ✿ Does she begin to stack blocks independently?

Tips

- ✿ Provide blocks of different textures or sizes for baby to explore.
- ✿ If you are having trouble getting baby interested in the stacking game, place unexpected objects on the stack, like a toy car or animal figure. How does baby react? Laugh or otherwise show baby that you are being silly. Then invite baby to try stacking, either with the silly object or with a block.

Motor 🖐

12+ months

Anywhere

Prep Time ⏱ **5 minutes**

Benefits
- ✿ Develops fine motor skills
- ✿ Promotes understanding of cause and effect

Materials
- ☑ Blocks

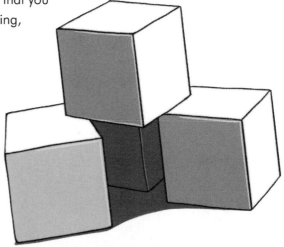

Through the Tube

What to do

1. Hold the tube near baby, and drop a small toy through it so that it comes out the other side. Continue doing this until the child reaches for it.
2. Hold the tube up for the child, and invite him to drop objects through or otherwise explore the tube. **Note:** *If the child is still actively exploring objects with his mouth, pay careful attention to ensure he does not ingest bits of the paper tube.*

What to look for

* Does this activity keep the child's attention?
* Does he experiment with different objects to put in the tube?
* What else does he do with the paper towel tube and small objects?

Tips

* Try tubes of different sizes.
* Have a dowel rod or stick available to help children push objects through a longer tube.

Motor ✋

12+ months

Anywhere

Prep Time ⏲ **5 minutes**

Benefits
* Develops fine motor skills
* Promotes understanding of spatial relationships

Materials
* ☑ Paper towel tube
* ☑ Small toys to put through the tube (small cars, balls, scarves, and so on)

Feel the Hum

What to do

1. When an infant is fussy, hold her close to your neck and chest.
2. Hum a tune as you rock or walk with baby.

What to look for

✿ Does baby react to the sound or the vibrations that your vocal cords create?

Tips

✿ Record a family member singing a favorite lullaby to his child. Play this for baby to soothe her.
✿ Experiment with other sounds or movements that may calm baby. Some babies respond to music, while others are soothed by dull, continuous sounds such as that of a vacuum cleaner, fan, or blow-dryer.

Sensory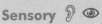

6 weeks+

Anywhere

Prep Time ⊕ **None**

Benefits
✿ Promotes auditory and tactile stimulation
✿ Soothes children

Materials
☑ None

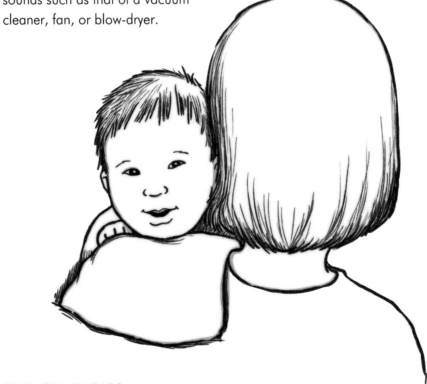

Crinkle, Crackle, Rip!

What to do

1. Give baby a large piece of tissue or butcher paper.
2. Encourage him to crinkle it up, shake it around, and tear it.

What to look for

* How does he grasp and manipulate the paper? Is he using his whole hand, or is he experimenting with his fingers? (Babies begin grasping and letting go when they are around three months old. This activity encourages this development.)
* Does he respond to the sounds of the paper crinkling and ripping?

Tips

* Use only white tissue paper or blank newsprint to prevent baby from getting stained when the paper gets wet.
* Supervise closely, and remove small ripped pieces to keep baby from ingesting them.

Sensory 👂 👁

3+ months

Anywhere

Prep Time ⏱ **5 minutes**

Benefits
* Promotes tactile and auditory stimulation
* Develops fine and gross motor skills

Materials
* ☑ White tissue paper or plain butcher paper

What's that Sound?

What to do

1. During tummy time (see page 9 for more information about tummy time), or any other time when baby is lying down, hold a sound-making object near baby's head but out of baby's view. For example, if baby is on her tummy with her head turned to the right, hold the object to the left of her head.
2. Rattle, shake, or otherwise make a sound with the object.
3. When baby turns to look for the sound, make the noise again so that she can see where it came from.
4. Move the object out of view, and make the noise again.
5. Continue for as long as the child is interested.

What to look for

✿ Does baby react to the sound when you first make it?
✿ Does she turn her head to seek out the sound?
✿ If she is on her tummy, does she lift her head or upper body to look for the object?

Tips

✿ Move the object as baby begins looking for it. Does she track the sound? Do this only for a short time and then show her the object to avoid frustrating the baby.
✿ Try this with different objects that make different kinds of sounds. Is there one that baby reacts to more quickly or with more enthusiasm?

Sensory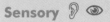

3+ months

Anywhere

Prep Time �🕐 **5 minutes**

Benefits
✿ **Promotes auditory stimulation**
✿ **Encourages gross motor development**

Materials
☑ **Any object that makes a sound**

Watch the Wind

What to do

1. Hang the wind catchers around your outdoor space where infants can easily see them.
2. On breezy days take baby outdoors to experience the wind catchers moving.

What to look for

- Does baby react to the feel of the wind on her skin?
- Does she notice the movement of the wind catchers on her own?
- Does baby reach for the wind catchers as you approach them?

Tips

- Hang light scarves over the outdoor area where nonmobile infants lie, so that they too can watch the movement of the wind.
- In addition to wind catchers, hang wind chimes outdoors for added sensory stimulation.
- If baby is sensitive to the wind, or it is too cold to go outdoors, watch the wind catchers through a window.

Sensory

3+ months

Outdoors

Prep Time 10 minutes

Benefits
- Promotes sensory stimulation (visual and tactile)
- Encourages gross motor development

Materials
- Weatherproof flags, banners, or other wind catchers

Creeping Crawlers

What to do

1. In a large open area, secure each textured surface to the floor using tape. Make sure that each surface is touching at least one other surface.
2. Invite children to crawl across the pathway or space you have created.

What to look for

✿ How does baby react to the changes in texture? Does he show a preference?
✿ Does the child find small cracks or bumps to explore more closely?

Tips

✿ Even nonmobile infants can experience tummy time (see page 15 for more information about tummy time) on some of these surfaces by exploring the textures with their fingers. Just make sure that they are protected from more mobile children.
✿ Try this activity outdoors, and use natural surfaces such as grass and sand to enhance the experience.

Sensory 🦻 👁

6+ months

Anywhere

Prep Time 🕐 **10 minutes**

Benefits
✿ Promotes tactile stimulation
✿ Develops fine and gross motor skills

Materials
☑ Variety of textured surfaces (carpet squares; large pieces of corrugated cardboard; large sheets of bubble wrap; silicone mats; contact paper, sticky side up; and so on)
☑ Tape

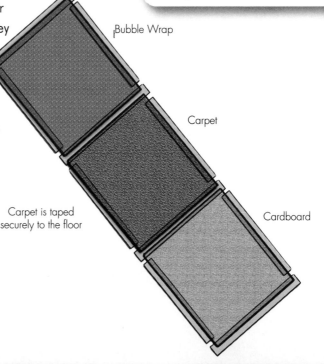

Bubble Wrap

Carpet

Cardboard

Carpet is taped securely to the floor

Rockin' Rhythms

What to do

1. Set baby down with a container turned upside-down, and give her a spoon.
2. Hit the container with the spoon to make a sound. Encourage her to do the same.
3. Invite her to experiment with other spoons and other containers.

What to look for

- Is baby able to coordinate her movements to hit the objects with the spoon?
- How does baby react to the sounds she makes?
- Does the child find other ways to experiment with the containers and spoons?

Tips

- Try this activity outdoors where the noise may be less bothersome.
- Make other rhythm instruments available to the children (xylophones, drums, maracas, and so on).
- Challenge children by giving them small containers to hit. This develops eye-hand coordination.

Sensory 👂 👁

6+ months

Anywhere

Prep Time 🕐 **5 minutes**

Benefits
- Promotes auditory stimulation
- Develops gross motor skills
- Develops understanding of cause and effect

Materials
- ☑ Variety of nonbreakable containers (plastic food containers, shoeboxes, metal pots, and so on)
- ☑ Variety of large spoons (wooden, metal, plastic)

Splish Splash!

Sensory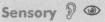

6+ months

Messy Area or Outdoors

Prep Time ⏱ 5 minutes

What to do

1. Cover the bottom of a shallow tray with water.
2. Invite baby to explore the water, splashing, slapping, and swishing his hands and arms around. **Note:** *Never leave baby unattended around water.*

What to look for

✿ How does baby react to the feel of the water?
✿ How does he react to the sound or movement of the water?

Tips

✿ Elevate the tray slightly to prevent baby from crawling into it. Supervise baby closely.
✿ Experiment with warm and cold water.
✿ Older infants can develop their fine motor skills by playing with a small sponge in the water.

Benefits

✿ Promotes sensory stimulation (tactile and auditory)
✿ Develops gross motor skills
✿ Promotes understanding of cause and effect

Materials

☑ Water
☑ Shallow tray

A World of Color

What to do

1. Hold a plastic sheet close to your face, and look at baby.
2. Hold the sheet near baby's face.
3. Give it to baby to explore.

What to look for

- Does baby hold the plastic sheet to her face?
- Does she react to how it changes the way things look?

Tips

- Talk about the color of the plastic.
- Tape one or more plastic sheets to a window at child height. Invite children to look out onto the red, blue, or yellow world.
- Set out a variety of colors for older infants to explore.

Sensory 👂 👁

9+ months

Indoors

Prep Time 🕐 **5 minutes**

Benefits
- Provides visual stimulation

Materials
- ☑ Colored transparent plastic sheets (report covers work well)
- ☑ Tape

Mold It, Mash It

What to do

1. Set baby in a high chair or at a low table. Placing baby on the floor with a tray also works well. Give him a small portion of dough.
2. Encourage baby to explore, squish, and poke the dough. The dough will not harm him if ingested, but try not to let him bite off chunks.

What to look for

✿ How does baby react to the texture?
✿ How does he manipulate or explore the dough? Does he do so with his whole hand? fingers?
✿ What other sensory responses does he have? Is he interested in the smell? the taste?

Tips

✿ If baby is not interested in grabbing the dough, set it on the table or tray. Flatten it a bit, and poke it with your fingers. Encourage him to put his fingers in the holes you have made.
✿ Make sure baby has a full belly to discourage him from eating the dough.
✿ Supervise baby closely to prevent choking if baby ingests a bit of dough.
✿ Older infants may enjoy using simple tools such as sticks, mallets, or spoons to manipulate the dough.

Sensory 👂 👁

12+ months

Messy Area

Prep Time ⏱ **5 minutes**

Benefits
✿ **Promotes tactile stimulation**
✿ **Develops fine motor skills**

Materials
☑ **Cloud Dough (see next page) or other oily playdough**

Cloud Dough

What to do

1. Mix together the flour and oil.
2. Add the water, and knead the dough together. You may need more water to make the dough bind.
3. When the dough is smooth and oily, you are done!
4. Store it in an airtight container.

Variations

✿ Add a small amount of food coloring for more visual appeal.

Prep Time ⏱ **10 minutes**

Ingredients
3 cups flour
½ cup cooking oil
½ cup water

Fingerpainting Fun

 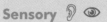

What to do

1. Set baby in a high chair or at a low table.
2. Squeeze a small amount of paint onto the tabletop or tray.
3. Show baby how to move his fingers through the paint to make marks on the tray.
4. Encourage him to experiment with and explore the paint.

What to look for

✿ How does baby react to the feel of the paint?
✿ How does he respond to the marks his fingers leave behind?

Tips

✿ Have wet wipes or paper towels nearby to wipe baby clean before he moves on to another activity.
✿ Invite baby to help you clean up with a damp cloth or paper towels.
✿ Avoid using this activity with infants who are still actively exploring their environment with their mouths.

12+ months

Messy Area

Prep Time ⏱ **5 minutes**

Benefits
✿ Promotes tactile stimulation
✿ Develops fine motor skills

Materials
☑ Nontoxic fingerpaint (one color)
☑ Large tray or tabletop

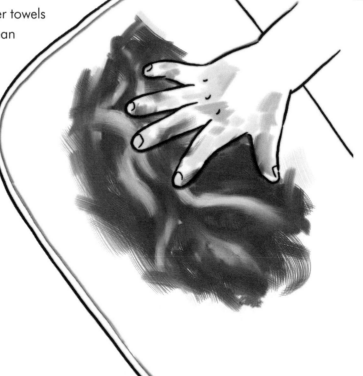

Fingerpaint Recipe

What to do

1. Place all ingredients in a bowl and stir. The dish detergent gives the paint a silky texture and makes cleanup a little easier, but it is not necessary. Leave it out if you are concerned about children ingesting the paint.
2. Use a handheld blender for very smooth paint, or stir it quickly with a spoon for a more bumpy texture.
3. Transfer the paint to a squeeze bottle, or store it in an airtight container and spoon it out as needed.

Variations

✿ Add sawdust or sand for a different texture.
   Note: *Omit if it is likely that the paint will be ingested.*

Prep Time ⊕ **10 minutes**

Ingredients
1 cup flour
1 cup water
Food coloring
1/8 cup liquid dish
   detergent (optional)

Note: Although adding dish detergent makes the paint easier to clean up, omit this ingredient if it is likely that the paint will be ingested.

Touch and Turn Wheel

What to do

1. Tape the shapes onto the turntable.
2. Invite the children to watch what happens (if you used colored paper) or to touch the shapes and spin the turntable.

What to look for

- ✿ Can children spin the turntable independently?
- ✿ How do they react to the colors or the various textures?

Tips

- ✿ Have small toys handy for children to place on the turntable. Invite children to explore what happens to the toys when the turntable spins.
- ✿ Make different turntable patterns by arranging the shapes or items differently.

Sensory 🦻 👁️

12+ months

Anywhere

Prep Time 🕐 **20 minutes**

Benefits
- ✿ **Promotes visual and tactile stimulation**
- ✿ **Develops fine motor skills**
- ✿ **Develops understanding of cause and effect**

Materials
- ☑ **Lazy Susan or kitchen turntable**
- ☑ **Tape**
- ☑ **Large shapes cut from colored paper or textured items (sand paper, fabric, cotton batting, and so on)**

Hear and Seek

What to do

1. Hide the noisy object somewhere nearby.
2. Ask the children to listen carefully. Can they hear that sound? Where is it coming from?
3. Have an adult help the children find the source of the sound.

What to look for

❀ Do the children move in the direction of the sound?
❀ Do they communicate or help one another?
❀ If they have trouble at first, do they catch on after you show them how to follow the sound?

Tips

❀ If the children are not motivated to find the object, ask another adult or an older child to hide with a noisy toy. Ask that person to play with the toy until the children find her.
❀ Hide the object under a cloth or in a box as the child watches. Encourage her to uncover or find it.

Sensory 👂 👁

12+ months

Anywhere

Prep Time 🕐 **5 minutes**

Benefits
❀ Develops listening skills
❀ Promotes problem-solving skills
❀ Encourages social skills

Materials
☑ Loud ticking clock, portable radio, or other noisemaking object

Index